DR JOHN CLARKE has completed studies and research in psychology in the areas of psychopaths in the workplace, criminal profiling, serial rape, animal cruelty offenders and sexual homicide crime scene analysis. He works as a consultant to corporations experiencing problems with a suspected workplace psychopath, as well as with victims of workplace psychopaths. He has also worked as a consultant for the NSW Police in developing offender profiles. He has lectured on psychopaths in the workplace, criminal profiling, abnormal psychology and criminal psychology at the University of Sydney, as well as to members of various law enforcement agencies, legal practitioners and psychologists. John has commented on criminal psychology and workplace psychopaths in print media, radio and television, both in Australia and overseas. Further information on workplace psychopaths and related topics can be found at www.drjohnclarke.com.

The Pocket Psycho

Dr John Clarke

RANDOM HOUSE AUSTRALIA

For Courtney

Random House Australia Pty Ltd
Level 3, 100 Pacific Highway, North Sydney, NSW 2060
www.randomhouse.com.au

Sydney   New York   Toronto
London   Auckland   Johannesburg

First published by Random House Australia 2007
Copyright © John Clarke 2007

National Library of Australia
Cataloguing-in-Publication Entry

Clarke, John, 1976–.
The pocket psycho.

ISBN 978 1 74166 488 1.

1. Psychopaths. 2. Antisocial personality disorders. 3. Bullying in the workplace – Prevention.
4. Intimidation – Prevention. I. Title.

658.3145

Cover image by Getty Images
Cover design by Darian Causby/www.highway51.com.au
Typeset by Midland Typesetters, Australia
Printed and bound by Griffin Press

Contents

Introduction

KATE MADE A decision to throw herself from a cliff because she could no longer stand being slowly destroyed by a workplace psychopath. A week earlier, her husband, who had read my book *Working with Monsters*, had contacted me, desperately trying to arrange for her to see me. Unfortunately, by the time arrangements were made to see Kate it was too late.

I have had an overwhelming response to *Working with Monsters*, which provided an in-depth look at the workplace psychopath. I receive a huge number of emails each week from people all over the world asking me to help them deal with workplace psychopaths in their lives. Because I cannot respond to every request that I receive, I decided to write *The Pocket Psycho* to provide as many people as I can with a brief, easily digested, user-oriented guide to the workplace psycho-path. While *Working with Monsters* combined scientific theory with practical advice, *The Pocket Psycho* provides specific infor-mation on how to deal with the workplace psychopath.

The aim of this book is to educate people about how the workplace psychopath operates. Education is the key to min-imising the harm these people cause. Once you know how they operate, they are much easier to deal with. *The Pocket Psycho* is intended for the wide range of people who are directly and indirectly affected by a workplace psychopath. It is hoped that people working for or with a workplace psychopath, friends and colleagues of people targeted by the workplace psychopath, people in a relationship with a work-place psychopath, and people in positions of power to do something about the workplace psychopath will all benefit from the information in this book.

We shall explore how the workplace psychopath operates, at both the strategic and day-to-day levels, as well as proven management strategies for minimising their effect in the organisation. We shall also look closely at the workplace psychopath's key characteristics. For victims, knowledge is power. It is vital that victims (and their relatives and col-leagues) realise that they are not going crazy or overreacting, that what they are experiencing is genuine and highly significant. Victims should also know that they are not alone. The workplace psychopath tries to isolate and then destroy a target. If you are a victim, read this book and know that you are not alone. The workplace psychopath will find it far more difficult to target you if you are well informed. You have taken the first step towards empowering yourself.

If *The Pocket Psycho* makes it more difficult for a psychopath to target victims and destroy people's lives, it has succeeded. If it saves the life of someone like Kate and improves the lives of victims like those who contact me, it has succeeded beyond measure.

However, the book is not intended to be used as a diagnostic tool for readers to classify their boss or colleague as a psychopath. Instead, it shows what a workplace psychopath is and demonstrates that they can be dealt with in a number of ways. It may be appropriate to seek professional advice if any situations identified in the book are similar to a situation you or someone you know is experiencing.

Further information on survivor support groups, research papers, scientific information and other material related to the workplace psychopath can be found at my website, www.drjohnclarke.com.

1

The Facts

THE ORGANISATIONAL PSYCHOPATH seeks power and control over others, thriving on the suffering and misery inflicted upon co-workers. They manipulate people and corporations at will, leaving a trail of devastation and broken colleagues in their wake. They are found in all types of organisation, working at every level from chief executive to junior employee.

Mary was a mid-level manager in an insurance firm. She could manipulate any situation, no matter how bad, so that she ended up looking successful. She lied to both colleagues and clients, but never took responsibility when her deception was exposed. She would simply turn on her charm and ingratiate herself with senior management, laying the blame directly on someone else. Her mood swings were completely unpredictable; one minute she was nice and the next she would turn on colleagues, causing many people in the organisation to fear her. Perhaps what struck her colleagues most was her complete lack of remorse or guilt when caught doing something wrong.

Mary would do whatever it took to look good at the expense of her colleagues. Mary is an organisational psychopath.

Despite increased public awareness in recent years, organisational psychopaths like Mary still operate with impunity. They show a distinct cluster of personality characteristics, as well as antisocial behaviours. These characteristics and behaviours include a lack of remorse or guilt, parasitic behaviour, seeking increased power and control in the organisation, manipulating and intimidating the people around them, self-importance, an impersonal sex life, prolific lying and deception, a constant need for excitement, superficial charm, and a lack of responsibility.

Not all organisational psychopaths display every characteristic. What is important is the psychopath's pattern of behaviour. Their behaviour is shaped by how they think about the world and their workplace. They do not see work as a place to co-operate with colleagues and be productive;

rather, it is viewed as a place to manipulate and control co-workers and 'win' promotion to a position of greater power.

When faced with a workplace psychopath's destructive behaviour, victims characteristically report feeling as though they have lost control over their lives. Panic attacks, depression, disturbed sleep and nightmares, relationship problems, confusion, disbelief, guilt, lack of trust, anger, powerlessness, flashbacks, shame, embarrassment and sexual dysfunction are just a few examples of how these victims suffer.

Some longer-term effects also include being unable to look for another job, as they do not trust people or themselves anymore, and a loss of confidence in their ability to perform adequately in their chosen profession or career.

Employees who choose to stay in the workplace despite the trauma frequently report feeling resentment toward the company they have given so much to; they believe it has let them down by not believing or protecting them.

Some statistics

It is estimated that 1 to 3 per cent of adult males and 0.5 to 1 per cent of adult females are psychopaths. It is difficult to know how many organisational psychopaths are out there because they are masters at hiding themselves within an organisation. Moreover, employers are not forthcoming when it comes to revealing how many psychopaths they may have employed. However, researchers around the world believe that 1 per cent of the working adult population are organisational psychopaths. Dr Paul Babiak and Dr Robert Hare, leading workplace psychopath researchers in the USA, estimate that psychopathic individuals make up much more than 1 per cent of business managers and executives, and this appears to describe the Australian situation accurately as well.

According to Drs Babiak and Hare, a further 10 per cent of the population cannot be diagnosed as organisational psychopaths but still display enough psychopathic traits to have a significant negative impact on the people they encounter through their work.

Characteristics

The organisational psychopath is difficult to identify based on initial impressions. They are expert at manipulating people and situations so they elude detection, for a long time in many cases. The organisational psychopath uses a range of strategies to enter an organisation. Once they have secured a position they use a different set of tactics to accelerate their promotion within the company. The corporate reconnaissance and organisational manipulation tactics employed by the organisational psychopath often lead to discovery by the organisation and conflict between the organisation and the psychopath. However, the psychopath can become such a senior member of the company that conflict either does not occur or becomes virtually impossible to resolve.

The organisational psychopath targets a number of different victim types. These victim types depend on perceived usefulness of the victim to the organisational psychopath, as well as the level of power and influence the victim has within the organisation. Potential victims can significantly minimise their risk of being manipulated by an organisational psychopath by increasing their knowledge of strategies used by the psychopath.

The workplace psychopath is, of course, very difficult for an organisation to manage. But there are a number of management strategies that can be employed, and used wisely they can be extremely effective. We shall explore these strategies later in this book.

Born or made?

There is some controversy about whether an organisational psychopath is created by nature (born) or nurture (environment), or a combination of the two. The idea that it is a combination of genes, biology and the environment that produces the psychopathy syndrome has a great deal of resonance.

Psychopathy is a lifelong condition. It is a personality disorder; therefore characteristics are consistently displayed across all aspects of a psychopath's life. However, psychopaths are expert at hiding these negative characteristics behind what psychiatrist Dr Harvey Cleckley called a 'mask of sanity'.

Mad or bad?

Organisational psychopaths, and psychopaths in general, are not mad. The organisational psychopath is essentially bad. They are aware of the effect their behaviours have on the people around them – they just do not care. Worse, a number of organisational psychopaths enjoy the suffering of the people around them.

Can they be cured?

'Rehabilitating' the organisational psychopath is a difficult proposition at best. While little research has examined organisational psychopaths, studies of violent criminal psychopaths suggest rehabilitation programs can actually make the psychopath worse. The psychopath can develop new social skills that they then use to manipulate people more effectively.

What can be done?

The most effective strategy that can be employed when dealing with the organisational psychopath is to have a detailed knowledge of how they operate. Once the psychopath's modus operandi is understood, it becomes much simpler to predict and to some extent control their behaviours.

This book aims to provide you with the understanding and knowledge of the organisational psychopath necessary to give you a far greater chance of recognising and dealing with a psychopath in the workplace.

2

Defining the Monster

THE ORGANISATIONAL PSYCHOPATH derives gratification from psychologically destroying co-workers. There are two objectives for many organisational psychopaths. The first objective is to get to the top for the financial rewards and the power the position brings.

David worked for a large insurance company, and had a variety of techniques and devious strategies that helped him get promoted. Among other things, he would steal co-workers projects so he looked better than they did, he would spread false rumours about his boss, and he lied to clients to make sure he got the contract and then passed the work on to someone else who would get the blame when services were not delivered as he had promised. David was seen by the executive team as an up-and-coming star in the company. Most people had no idea that he had ruthlessly achieved his numerous promotions at the expense of the people around him.

The second objective for psychopaths is to revel in the suffering and misery they inflict on the people they work with.

Mark was a senior manager of the Australian division of a multinational company. He had read about my consulting work for companies with 'psychopathic' employees and organised a meeting, as he wanted to discuss a few things regarding his staff. Mark said that his employees were very unhappy and constantly under stress, and were resigning at unprecedented rates. Mark said he knew the cause of this: himself. He had deliberately implemented policies in the company to increase his staff's workload and stress levels because he enjoyed watching people trying to work under more pressure than they could cope with. He wanted me to tell him about strategies used by psychopaths I had seen so he could try those as well. Needless to say, I was stunned and terminated the meeting immediately. As part of my duty of care to the employees, I also requested a meeting with the Australian managing director and informed him about a potential reason for the company's high staff turnover rate. I believe Mark was transferred to an overseas division of the company for 'career development'.

The organisational psychopath can be the boss, an employee or a co-worker. They use an arsenal of psychological techniques designed to cause as much confusion and conflict as possible within the organisation.

A range of common behavioural and personality traits stand out amongst the organisational psychopaths I have observed in the course of my work in corporations.

These characteristics can be listed under the following broad areas:

- Organisational/Managerial Behaviour
- Interpersonal Behaviour
- Emotional/Individual Characteristics

Generally, the organisational/managerial conduct characteristics are typified by a desire for increased power and control within the company. This often creates conflict between other members of the organisation as they will do whatever it takes to get that power and control. The organisational psychopath takes delight in this conflict, as the atmosphere of confusion and hostility allows them to continue manipulating the situation for their own advantage.

> Anne was a senior executive in a marketing firm. Her behaviour was completely unpredictable. It shifted from looking at a specific contract to criticising her colleagues for no reason. She was impatient about anything that did not interest her, lacked focus for specific jobs (she would delegate to other people after failing to meet her own deadlines) and her co-workers could not rely on anything she said. One of the few things that you could rely on with Anne was that she would let you down somehow, and always avoid being criticised for her irresponsibility. Anne was also renowned for doing whatever it took to 'get the contract', no matter how unethical the behaviour, and then bullying her subordinates into doing the impossible. At the end of the process it always seemed to be Anne who looked good at the expense of those who actually did the work. She had an incredible ability to manipulate any situation so that she always came out looking successful.

The organisational psychopath's interpersonal conduct is marred by a general lack of trustworthiness. This behaviour is characterised by the common theme of power and control, a complete lack of consideration for other people's feelings, manipulative and intimidating behaviour, deceit and a devious charm. Interpersonal conduct revolves around serving the interests of the organisational psychopath, and any collateral damage caused to other people is either a bonus or of no concern.

> Luke was a bully when it came to dealing with his subordinates. He had no insight into how his behaviour made other people feel. He would shout at people, criticise them for his own mistakes and expect them to do things he knew were unreasonable. He would call them names and intimidate the newer members of his section, and he took delight in ruining the career of anyone who challenged him. Luke was not trusted by anyone in the office; it was common knowledge that anything he said was to be taken with a grain of salt because he would lie without hesitation. The people who worked for Luke felt trapped, as they needed his 'favourable ratings' for their careers to advance further. Luke took full advantage of the situation.

An unfeeling nature, a grandiose sense of self-worth, lack of remorse or guilt, self-importance, pathological lying, shallow emotions, sexual promiscuity and an impulsive nature are some of the emotional and individual characteristics of the organisational psychopath. These individual and emotional characteristics are the foundation for both the organisational/managerial and interpersonal behaviours.

Organisational Psychopath Characteristics

Organisational/ Managerial Behaviour	Interpersonal Behaviour	Emotional/Individual Characteristics
• Manipulative (at an organisational level)	• Manipulative (at an interpersonal level)	• Unfeeling
• Intolerant/easily bored	• Deceitful/devious/false	• Lacking a conscience
• Unethical behaviour	• No responsibility taken for own actions	• Grandiose/self-important
• Unpredictable/shallow emotions	• Intimidating	• Egocentric/narcissistic
• Parasitic behaviour	• Charming/superficial	• Shallow emotions
• Undependable		• Pathological lying
• Bullying (not necessarily confined to work)		• Marital problems
• Seek increased power and control in company		• Sexual promiscuity
• Create conflict between organisation members		• Impulsive

3

Specific Characteristics

As MENTIONED IN the previous section, organisational psychopaths have a number of distinct organisational/managerial, interpersonal, and individual/emotional factors that characterise both their behaviour and their approach towards everyday living.

Manipulative organisational and interpersonal behaviour

The organisational psychopath manipulates established social systems in the organisation to cause confusion, furthering their own career or destroying other people's. Organisational psychopaths will use deception in their manipulation of corporate systems and procedures to minimise their risk of being identified as 'manipulators'. They will also recruit unknowing and unwilling members of the company to help out with their manipulation of corporate politics. Organisational psychopaths may also manipulate select company personnel to create a situation advantageous to themselves.

James was a car salesman with ambition. He believed that he was ready for management (after working in the car yard for six months) and was prepared to do whatever it took to get there. James engineered a situation where his fellow workers began to feel used by the management staff, and sales fell as the discontent grew. James continually stirred up the workers' dissatisfaction, constantly creating rumours about management business trips and spending sprees while the salespeople's own base salaries had not changed due to the 'financial downturn'.

At the same time, James was liaising with management and undermining his co-workers. Management began to trust James because his advice about the colleagues he was spying on proved to be accurate. James was eventually made team leader in charge of his colleagues. He made work conditions so unpleasant for some of his former 'friends' that they decided to leave. James took control over his workmates and sales rose again, making James look good in the eyes of management. His workmates felt betrayed but could do nothing as management were already suspicious of them and trusted James implicitly.

Unethical behaviour

Accepted moral and professional codes of conduct mean nothing to the organisational psychopath. They will promise more than they are able to deliver, blackmail people to get contracts and to look good in their own company, have sexual relationships with people they have authority or influence over, put in false company records to show work completed that they have not done, and take credit for other people's work. Loopholes in the law are exploited to the full. Generally, they see the world as an opportunity, and they will take what they want regardless of the expense to other people. If rules or codes of conduct need to be broken in order to achieve their aims, so be it.

Dr William Harrison was well known amongst criminals and drug users as being willing to provide false medical certificates and drugs. Dr Harrison demanded only two things of patients he provided special services for – sexual favours and cocaine or ecstasy. Dr Harrison was not a drug user; he simply had an extravagant party lifestyle to support (including a number of mistresses) and sold the drugs he obtained to his friends.

Intolerant/easily bored

The organisational psychopath becomes bored with and intolerant towards situations and people very quickly. They also display very low patience for dealing with the everyday problems and issues facing their staff or fellow workers. In fact, they often see fellow staff as beneath them, and not worth wasting time on unless it provides the organisational psychopath with some pleasure or career benefit. They like to create excitement and stimulation for themselves, whether that be through engineering a crisis or taking a risk with company funds. They may move frequently between jobs as their work routine becomes monotonous, or they may take on a number of roles within the one workplace to ensure constant stimulation. However, taking on a number of jobs or roles in the one company does not mean any one job will be completed. The organisational psychopath rarely finishes anything; they usually 'delegate' to other people or talk their way out of a situation where work has not been produced as promised.

> Sharon was the employee welfare co-ordinator in a large government department. She was intolerant and became bored extremely easily, dismissing employee welfare issues as they did not interest her. (She had taken the job because it was close to home and allowed her to be away from the office unsupervised.) Sharon neglected her duties to such an extent that an employee who had been involved in an extremely traumatic event attempted to kill himself after repeated requests to Sharon for help in the form of counselling. Sharon could not understand why she was reprimanded and had absolutely no remorse for not doing her job, as it 'bored her'. She saw the person who tried to kill himself as weak in a world where one had to be strong.

Unpredictable behaviour/shallow emotions

The organisational psychopath is commonly seen as impulsive and erratic in their behaviour. They constantly shift between projects so that their co-workers never know what is happening at any one time. This means that people can never work out what projects the psychopath is working on, or whether a job is finished properly. Such confusion also allows this type of psychopath to survive, without being discovered, in a constantly changing workplace. The unpredictable nature of the organisational psychopath is closely linked to shallow emotions. The ability to rapidly shift between emotions to correspond with a situation confuses others, allowing the psychopath to deflect attention away from an issue that could reflect negatively on themselves. This sort of behaviour causes fear amongst people who work with the organisational psychopath, as they never know what to expect. This leaves the victims of an organisational psychopath helpless and increases their overall stress levels in the workplace – exactly what the organisational psychopath wants.

Parasitic behaviour

The organisational psychopath is generally a parasite when it comes to surviving and flourishing in the workplace. Parasitic behaviour includes taking credit for other people's work, conning other people into doing their own work, and 'delegating' all their work to junior staff. There are three main ways the organisational psychopath is able to have other people complete their work for them. First, they may use intimidation and threats to coerce a fellow employee into doing their work. Second, they identify a weak or vulnerable person and deliberately prey on their weak points to manipulate them. Finally, they may present themselves as being helpless or deserving of compassion or sympathy, emotionally blackmailing fellow workers into taking on their duties. The organisational psychopath has no consideration for the strain his or her parasitic behaviour imposes on fellow employees. In fact, as we have seen, some organisational psychopaths in more senior positions *enjoy* putting extra stress on their employees. Parasitic behaviour is not only confined to the workplace. Often friends and family will be exploited, for example, asking for 'loans' that are never repaid or encouraging parents to mortgage their house so they can indulge themselves.

Cheryl was a schoolteacher who displayed many psychopathic characteristics, one of which was parasitic behaviour. She never prepared any lessons; instead, she would 'borrow' lesson plans from other teachers at the school. When the principal commented on the high quality of her lessons, Cheryl replied that the other teachers at the school agreed and had asked if they could borrow her lesson plans. Cheryl would encourage parents to do personal favours for her, such as free car washes and repairs, small home repairs, discounted travel, and so on. Cheryl would also make more junior teachers mark her students' homework as part of her 'supervision' of their early careers. Generally, Cheryl had people do everything for her and took credit for everything herself.

Undependable and failure to take responsibility for behaviour

Nothing is ever the organisational psychopath's fault; it is always someone else or a breakdown in communication. If a person depends on the organisational psychopath they are highly likely to be let down, at great personal expense to themselves. The psychopath will generously volunteer for projects that will make them look good, and consistently fail to complete their side of the deal. When client contracts are not fulfilled, the organisational psychopath will attempt to avoid responsibility by minimising the consequences, saying such things as 'that is just business' and 'it is survival of the fittest,' if they were stupid enough to believe we could fill such an unrealistic contract, they deserve everything they get'.

Being undependable at work can be seen in continual lateness, poor or careless work performance, frequent sick leave and promising to do work that never gets done. Letting people down is usually observed in more than just a work situation; for example, defaulting on loan payments, poor credit history, non-payment of child support, 'forgetting' to pick up the children from school, and so on. Responsibility for poor performance or letting co-workers down is denied no matter what evidence exists. Organisational psychopaths frequently direct attention away from themselves.

Amongst other characteristics of organisational psychopathy, Scott frequently failed to show up for work until well after his starting times. He would miss important meetings, saying he was busy doing other business deals and did not have time for the mundane, day-to-day matters the company involved itself in. He denied that he was incompetent or lazy despite never producing anything. He claimed that everyone in the company had it in for him and frequently 'could not remember' what events people were talking about when he was accused of not performing satisfactorily at work. Scott caused the people he worked with to appear unprofessional; they frequently had to cover for his absences or risk losing their bonuses, for the company was structured in such a way as to pay the team (rather than individuals) for work well done.

Workplace bullying

Bullying is repeated behaviour that is intended to make another person feel bad, or to cause physical injury. Psychological bullying carried out by the organisational psychopath can include social isolation, humiliation, verbal abuse, unwarranted criticism, intrusive supervision, records being made in personnel files that are unjustified, singling out people for different treatment, physical threats and violence. Organisational psychopaths will often go to great lengths to isolate and bully vulnerable individuals; often, they then create a protective 'culture of silence', which allows them to continue such behaviour unchecked.

It is not uncommon for organisational psychopaths to bully other people in their lives, particularly family members.

However, they can camouflage their bullying so well that family friends and management in the workplace often do not believe that the offender actually is a bully. I have seen numerous cases in which such people have actually defended the organisational psychopath's behaviour without realising the extent of the problem until irrefutable evidence was presented. Unfortunately, the delay in presenting such evidence generally means that victims suffer for longer.

Denise was a 23-year-old customer service assistant in a large restaurant chain. She was referred to me by a friend and felt her life was falling to pieces as a result of being bullied at work by Susan, a 21-year-old trainee manager. Denise presented with extremely high anxiety levels and reported behaviours that bordered on showing signs of a depressive episode. Susan constantly picked on Denise for no particular reason. She would continually criticise Denise's work without justification and would humiliate her in front of both customers and other staff. Susan could not respond, having been threatened with the loss of her job, something she could not afford as she had purchased a car recently and had to keep up the repayments. Denise's shifts were constantly rescheduled at very short notice, and she was never given overtime.

Susan continually asked Denise how she ever got a job there, implying that the job was well above Denise's capabilities. Denise was given all the unpleasant jobs; whenever anyone was sick or the toilets needed cleaning, Denise would be the first person called if Susan was on duty. In fact, Denise was given so many additional tasks that she could not complete them all, at which point she was called in by Susan and verbally abused for not doing her job. Denise was told in no uncertain terms that if she found the work too difficult she should leave.

Susan lied to the other managers in the store about Denise, so that none of them would give her a reference. She was effectively trapped in a position that was intolerable. The stress of the situation became so unbearable that Denise was forced to sell her car and quit her job. She felt that she would never be able to work for another person again. Susan had lowered Denise's self-esteem to such a point that Denise had no confidence in herself whatsoever. It took months of counselling before Denise felt comfortable to start looking for other jobs.

Seek increased power and control in the company

The organisational psychopath lives for power and control over other people. It makes them feel 'godlike' to know that they hold the fate of other people in their hands and there is nothing that their victims can do about the situation. Having the ability to allocate duties to other staff, to hire and fire staff, to direct the company business strategies in their own favour, to earn more money and be viewed as important, and to be allocated private staff to cater to their personal needs all feed this sense of power and control. They do not care so much about other people's opinions of them, and they are not necessarily proud of their increased influence within the company. It is the sense of 'owning' other people that is important for them, along with the challenge of gaining even more power and control in their workplace. The organisational psychopath constantly engages in manipulative strategies and devious, unethical conduct to continue their rise through the organisation's ranks. This climb to the top stimulates the organisational psychopath – the 'thrill of the hunt'. This thrill is similar to the thrill felt by the violent criminal psychopath when they are anticipating the crime they will commit. But instead of physically possessing victims as a violent criminal psychopath does, the organisational psychopath psychologically possesses and sometimes destroys people.

Create conflict between organisation members

It is often said that there is strength in numbers. If the organisational psychopath can create conflict between co-workers, it allows them to control their co-workers more easily. The psychopath also finds it satisfying to see people insulting and hurting each other. Generally, conflict is created using two simple strategies.

The first is to select a co-worker who is different from everyone else. This difference may be a physical feature or a personality characteristic (extreme introverts are a favoured target as they are least likely to provide any resistance). The psychopath then manipulates his or her co-workers to ostracise the 'different' person. The victim obviously resists this treatment and there is conflict between the outsider and others in the work group. Depending on how strong the victim is, the conflict can last for a long period of time. This satisfies the psychopath as the attention on them is conveniently deflected.

Some organisational psychopaths become 'leaders' by continually instigating the harassment and developing allies in the workplace. These allies can be used to create more conflict. They also provide a power base of support for the psychopath in his or her efforts to be promoted.

The second strategy used to create conflict is to spread rumours about other employees. Using the false rumours, the organisational psychopath will create the impression that they have inside information. Managers who are organisational psychopaths will often use rumours to encourage intense competition between team members. This works to safeguard their own position by directing attention toward positions junior to their own.

Louise was a real estate agent working in a suburban office. She was a junior salesperson and wanted a bigger role in the company; she resented others earning more money than she did when she 'knew' that they could never be as good as her. Louise was very attractive and flirted with the salesmen in the office. Louise also invented rumours about another saleswoman, Natalie, who had worked in the office for years. She hoped to make life so unpleasant for Natalie that she would leave and Louise would get her job and salary.

Louise pretended to be friends with Natalie, and told her that she should complain that Greg, another salesman in the office, was stealing her clients. Very soon, Greg and Natalie disliked each other, and the rest of the office was dragged into their conflict as well. Louise simply watched and manipulated each side to make sure the conflict continued. A once happy office was now extremely dysfunctional.

Deceitful/devious/frequent lying

Being deceitful and creating devious strategies in the workplace are a fundamental part of the organisational psychopath's interpersonal conduct. They can quickly work out what people want to hear, and create a story that corresponds with their listener's expectations. Their story is not necessarily well thought out, but the success of the deceit is often dependent on the organisational psychopath's superficial charm and ability to influence a group of people without the group realising what is really happening. Listeners are generally deceived by how the story is told rather than the story's content.

Intimidating behaviour

The organisational psychopath is usually able to identify how far they need to go in order to intimidate their co-workers. Psychological vulnerabilities are quickly identified and ruthlessly exploited. For example, a person who lacks self-confidence may be the subject of verbal ridicule by the psychopath in front of their co-workers because they dared to criticise or stand up to the psychopath. The organisational psychopath is not above making physical threats either. People who have experienced such a psychopath in the workplace have recounted that something about the psychopath was menacing, making them feel scared, as though the psychopath had far greater power and influence, and they did not dare to cross or upset them. This threat of intimidation is enhanced by co-workers seeing what happens to those who stand up to the psychopath. Victims eventually leave, are transferred to another section, become extremely miserable or are continually bullied by the psychopath. The one thing that co-workers find most alarming is the emotional detachment of the psychopath – their cold indifference and doing whatever is necessary to achieve their goal is truly frightening.

Charming/superficial

The organisational psychopath can be very charming, taking control of a conversation or group of people and leading them in any direction that serves the psychopath's needs. They will tell witty stories, know how to make people laugh (often at someone else's expense), and are generally very entertaining. Often the organisational psychopath appears to be knowledgeable in a wide range of areas. When caught out by a more informed listener, they are unfazed and will change the topic or encourage their critic to expand on their subject area so the psychopath will not be caught out the next time. The psychopath might bully their way through a conversation, and by sheer force of their charm and personality, people will believe them. If questioned about their facts, the organisational psychopath will attempt to steer the conversation in another direction. When the organisational psychopath's lack of knowledge is found out, they show very little if any concern, and gloss over the gap in their story by reworking the facts. Some organisational psychopaths are very proud of their ability to persuade people to do things they would not normally do by using their charm and good communication skills.

The criteria presented above are general characteristics that one would expect to see in an organisational psychopath. However, for people working with the organisational psychopath, it is not always possible to observe these characteristics on a daily basis. The following list provides some examples of behaviours that co-workers may observe in an organisational psychopath. The greater the number of behaviours displayed by the person of interest, the more urgent the need for a prompt and thorough investigation by an independent consultant. If multiple behaviours are observed, at the very least an internal assessment by the human resources department must be conducted.

Behaviours to be aware of include but are not limited to:

- Humiliates a person in public by shouting at them, temper tantrums, ridicule of work or physical disability
- Maliciously spreads lies about a person to discredit their reputation in the organisation
- Displays no remorse or guilt for their behaviour

- Frequently lies
- Rapidly shifts between emotions to manipulate people or cause high levels of fear
- Ignores a person to isolate them from organisational resources and support systems, making the victim feel socially isolated and helpless, increasing their vulnerability
- Accuses a person of making mistakes or not completing work when the accuser knows what they are saying is unfounded. This works to humiliate or shift blame away from the organisational psychopath who has failed to complete the work
- Encourages co-workers to torment, harass and humiliate a fellow co-worker
- Taking credit for other people's work
- Steals or sabotages a person's work so that the person is disciplined or embarrassed about completing assigned tasks
- Refuses to accept responsibility
- Uses the threats of job loss, disciplinary action, 'black marks' on personnel files as a way of intimidating others
- Sets unachievable tasks for employees to set them up for failure and allowing disciplinary action to be taken by them on behalf of the organisation

- Refuses to attend meetings when more than one person will be there as they do not want to be accused of not performing without being able to blame someone else
- Refuses to provide adequate training to a victim who has been singled out or targeted
- Invades the personal privacy of others by going through files, emails, desk contents
- Has multiple sexual encounters with junior and/or senior employees
- Develops new ideas and never follows through. Often these are given to someone at the last minute and the organisational psychopath will blame them when the new idea fails
- Self-focused, talk about themselves, act self-important, believe the world revolves around them
- May borrow sums of money from co-workers with no intention of ever repaying this money
- Does whatever it takes to secure a contract or deal, regardless of how unethical or illegal the behaviour may be

4

Manipulating Organisations

THE ORGANISATIONAL PSYCHOPATH manipulates organisations from the outset. The manipulation occurs at all stages of employment, starting when the psychopath applies for a job and continuing as they rise through the organisational ranks. Sometimes by the time the manipulation is discovered, the organisational psychopath is in such a powerful position that it is difficult to manage the situation. This costs the company enormous sums of money and can be devastating for people who work with or for the organisational psychopath.

How the psychopath selects their employer

Organisational psychopaths prefer positions in organisations that are undergoing change, restructuring or rapid expansion. These chaotic corporate environments make it easier for the psychopath to remain undetected for longer periods of time because they hide behind the organisational confusion. In some cases, the psychopath can even appear to be an up-and-coming employee because they steal other people's ideas and present them to upper management as their own.

Dianne was desperately trying to impress her boss, as people were starting to ask questions about her poor performance. She consistently failed to deliver work she was tasked with, and when she did it was of such poor quality that it had to be redone by someone else. Dianne used to talk to everyone she could in the office, pretending she was interested in their projects and complaining that the company did not allow for creative thinking and new ideas.

One worker, Ian, agreed with her, and as they discussed things and got to know each other better he confided in her that he had ideas for improvements in the organisation. Dianne listened intently, nodding and praising Ian and assuring him that she would keep his ideas to herself. Afterwards, Dianne immediately wrote a paper suggesting Ian's changes to upper management, who reviewed and loved the ideas.

Dianne was credited with being a fantastic worker, and her immediate boss was told to stop giving her a hard time as she was an 'employee on the rise' and needed to be given space for creativity. He was also told that not everybody could be as bright and creative as Dianne, and that if he was jealous of her he should leave rather than take it out on her.

When Dianne's boss and Ian confronted upper management and claimed that the ideas really belonged to Ian, they were told that it was 'pathetic' to try to steal credit for Dianne's ideas, and that people like them might be better suited to another organisation unless they behaved more professionally. Dianne not only succeeded in staying in the organisation, but also guaranteed protection from upper management for her poor work behaviour. Ian and Dianne's co-workers were divided over who came up with the ideas; Dianne had 'muddied the waters' so much that they did not know who or what to believe.

How the organisation selects the organisational psychopath

Generally, the employee selection process is fairly standard. Advertise the position, receive and screen résumés, interview prospective candidates who fit the selection criteria, do referee checks, and offer the job to the best candidate. Unfortunately, the organisational psychopath often appears to be the right person, because they have falsified their résumés and lied about themselves to best fit what the employer is looking for. Some job descriptions even advertise specifically for traits that the organisational psychopath has in abundance. Consider the following job advertisements:

You will be innovative with something special to offer. No doubt you will have leadership and influencing skills, and be able to WOW a sceptical selection panel. We want someone who can see the biggest picture and have broad impact. Your background could be in ... whatever, you will be someone special. Salary $150K+.

This was a senior management position in which the successful applicant could also quite easily steal on a large scale from the company.

You will have a strong desire to achieve, the capacity to persuade and influence others, excellent communication skills ... You want to work with the best. You enjoy competing as much as winning. You believe in high rewards for high levels of performance. Salary $85K.

This advertisement attracted an organisational psychopath who was ultimately recruited. If I were doing a study in which I needed to find organisational psychopaths, I would place advertisements similar to those above in the employment section of newspapers. In fact, some researchers in America did just that. They advertised for 'adventurous people who have led exciting lives ... charming people who are irresponsible but good at handling people'. They had a number of sub-criminal psychopaths reply to their advertisements.

It is clear from the advertisements above that glib and superficial charm, lack of remorse or guilt, and proneness to boredom are all characteristics that some corporations are advertising for. Obviously these corporations are not looking for a psychopath, however the advertisements they have placed may well appeal to the organisational psychopath, as well as non-psychopaths.

The job application and interview – entering the organisation

Contrary to what people imagine, the organisational psychopath finds it particularly easy to win positions in a wide range of companies. When it comes to recruitment, most companies either use a recruitment firm or hire employees directly. Employee selection is largely based on the quality of the applicants' résumés, verbal skills and impression management in the job interview, and sometimes referee checks. Performance in previous jobs is also analysed in some positions, however 'performance' usually refers to how much money, sales, accounts, and so on, the applicant was responsible for. Again, this information is often disclosed directly by the job applicant and is therefore able to be falsified as the previous employer is hardly likely to disclose such sensitive business information.

After the résumé screening process comes the interview phase. The organisational psychopath excels at this stage of the recruitment process. They use their charm and excellent verbal skills with tremendous effect, presenting a picture of the perfect candidate for the position.

Amy was an experienced human resources manager in a large pharmaceutical company. She wanted to know how she could prevent 'difficult employees' from being hired by her company, as it was extremely expensive and time-inefficient to monitor their behaviour and productivity.

Amy described one example in which 34-year-old Chris was hired as a sales manager. He was recommended by the recruitment firm as an 'outstanding' candidate, and he stood out in his final interview with Amy and some other experienced HR people; Amy recorded in her interview notes that he was 'a promising future leader in the company'. Chris seemed to anticipate questions the interviewers asked, answering each confidently and very well. He was obviously intelligent and outgoing, he claimed to be a team player, and based on his previous experience (about which he was not entirely truthful) he was a conscientious leader who would lift sales for the brand. Chris was offered the position.

After a few months, sales plummeted in Chris's team and his staff refused to work with him. (It was later discovered that Chris was passing on sensitive commercial information to the sales manager at a rival company, with whom he was having an affair.) Despite this, some senior managers liked him and saw him as a promising employee with a bright future. It was only after a trap involving sensitive company information was set that the senior managers realised what type of person Chris was and asked him to leave.

I advised Amy that there was no foolproof way to screen for such people, but that a number of basic checks should have been completed before hiring Chris.

Office politics and the organisational psychopath

The number and type of strategies used by the organisational psychopath to move their way up through the ranks varies. This is because the organisational psychopath is an intelligent, charming manipulator who reacts to each situation differently. The general aims of manipulative strategies implemented in the early stages of the organisational psychopath's career are threefold.

The first aim is to create disharmony between co-workers. In this confusion, the psychopath is able to play people against one another without them realising what is happening. Simultaneously, the organisational psychopath is able to endear themselves to management by resolving seemingly intractable situations. They demonstrate their leadership ability at the expense of their supervisor, who does not appear to be capable of resolving the situation created by the psychopath.

The second aim is to spread disinformation about rivals within the company. These rivals include co-workers at the same level as the psychopath as well as people in positions senior to the psychopath. Generally, this disinformation is spread through the use of third parties within the organisation. For example, the organisational psychopath may befriend a secretary or delivery person who has frequent contact with everyone in the organisation. The psychopath then tells this person a rumour, or series of rumours about a specific target, knowing that these rumours will rapidly spread around the organisation. They may also sabotage other people's work, palm off unachievable tasks to co-workers so that failure is inevitable, conceal problems from a supervisor until the last minute so the supervisor does not produce what is expected of them, and criticise a boss to senior management directly, ignoring the chain of command.

The third aim of the psychopath's manipulative strategies is impression management – to portray themselves in the best light possible. This is achieved by taking credit for other people's work (or even stealing it), creating crises and then 'saving the day' in a very noticeable way, exaggerating their achievements, bypassing the chain of command to impress senior managers directly, having third parties spread positive rumours about them, volunteering for extra projects and never completing them, searching for projects that will get them high exposure within the company, and cutting costs and overworking employees in the short term to secure a promotion without considering the fallout for the company.

However, it is important to note that the organisational psychopath does not treat all employees and co-workers in the same way. They selectively treat people according to how useful they consider them. This is where the importance of the manipulative strategy developed by the psychopath comes in to play. The level of sophistication differs between individual psychopaths, hence different levels of success are observed when looking at specific organisational psychopaths.

Dr Paul Babiak reports similar findings in American corporations who have experienced the organisational psychopath. In what Babiak calls the 'assessment' phase, the psychopath 'quickly assesses the utility of organisation members and can quickly charm them into being supporters. Co-workers' utility (to the psychopath) is based on position, power, technical abilities, access to information, and control of resources' (Babiak, 1995, p. 16). In other words, the organisational psychopath values powerful people, people able to do their work for them, people with access to information the psychopath needs, and people who control the corporate systems such as security guards (for building access) and auditors. Corporate systems are evaluated equally quickly by the psychopath for loopholes and avoidance mechanisms. They learn how to hide their behaviours, in addition to what they can 'get away with' in the organisation.

The organisational police

Workers whose role it is to check on employees, such as auditors, human resources and quality control personnel, are the natural enemy of the psychopath and very quickly detect the underlying nature of such individuals. They are not easily manipulated or conned, as they rely on hard cold figures to analyse what is going on rather than the psychopath's verbal promises of what will happen in the future. However, often when these people try to raise any concerns they are not listened to by those in authority because the organisational psychopath has already set up the foundations to protect their position.

Psychopathic corporations?

One interesting area concerns the similarity between corporate 'values' and psychopathy. Can the tactics and strategies used by organisations to achieve their goals be called psychopathic? If one goes through some of the psychopathy characteristics, a number of aspects of corporate behaviour may be considered 'psychopathic'.

However, given that a corporation is not one individual, corporations clearly cannot be diagnosed as psychopaths. The criteria are discussed to promote awareness of how a corporate culture may reflect certain values that are synonymous with psychopathy. Corporations in Western society are largely driven by competition, and the question needs to be asked: 'At what point does a win at all costs attitude and competitive behaviour resemble psychopathy?'

The characteristics listed below are intriguing to think about.

Glib and superficial

A number of organisations hire public relations and media consultants to create a certain image surrounding their company by using 'catchy' expressions and rather superficial terminology. For example, the majority of advertisements could be considered glib and superficial, showing customers all the positive aspects of a good or service and glossing over any bad aspects.

Egocentric and grandiose

Many organisations are self-focused and filled with a sense that they need to continue to grow and become 'market leaders' or the most important corporation in their market.

Lack of remorse or guilt

Corporations 'feel' the exact opposite of remorse or guilt when a competitor collapses or 'dies' as a result of their actions. The corporation views this as one less competitor in the marketplace that will result in them achieving greater market share. The 'death' of another corporation is seen as an

opportunity. Some corporations actively seek the economic collapse of competitors, doing everything they can to 'kill' their competitors financially.

Deceitful and manipulative

Corporations are not always honest. In fact, in some large corporations that have recently been investigated by government regulators, a culture of deception and manipulation of shareholders and customers appeared to be the 'norm'. It would be interesting to know how many other companies deceive shareholders and clients in the interest of 'making a profit'.

Parasitic

It could be construed as parasitic or living off other people's unfortunate circumstance when large multinationals 'exploit' poorly paid workers in third world countries. Many multinationals have factories in third world nations where their products are made at minimum cost (because they exploit very poor workers) and then sell these goods at significant profit levels in the Western world. Public opinion has made this practice less appealing from a public relations point of view. Some multinationals stopped using third world factories, and bought the same items from the same third world factories through sub-contractors so that the multinational could deny exploiting third world workers. This could be seen as manipulative and deceptive behaviour motivated by profit (or the 'self-gratification' of the company).

A paradox seems to exist between individual human versus corporate goals when it comes to co-existence and altruistic behaviour. Corporations are encouraged to compete with each other and win at all costs. In contrast, individuals are encouraged to work together in social networks, otherwise society would not function effectively. Corporations are encouraged to be driven by self-interest, individuals are encouraged to think about what is good for the society and put their own self-interests second to societal goals. Social cohesiveness is crucial to the survival of the human race.

Would it be possible for the human race to survive if every person on earth had the same values and attitudes as corporations do towards other corporations and customers?

5

Manipulating People

THE ORGANISATIONAL PSYCHOPATH is often regarded by those who first meet him or her as sincere, bright, a good communicator, and powerful. Some co-workers' opinions never change. The organisational psychopath never lets them see beneath the mask he or she presents to the world. Other co-workers are filled with fear and anger at the thought of the same psychopath. Organisational psychopaths use a series of tactics and complicated strategies to manage these discrepant views, facilitating their entry and subsequent rise in the company that unknowingly employed them.

Corporate reconnaissance and colleague appraisal

Once the organisational psychopath enters an organisation, they evaluate the people they will be working with, as well as the corporate systems that shape their working conditions. This is true of any new employee, psychopath and non-psychopath; it is natural to evaluate your new surroundings and co-workers. The organisational psychopath immediately tries to identify the usefulness of particular colleagues and loopholes in the corporate systems that will allow them to do what they want without interruption by the people who enforce company rules. The organisational psychopath also identifies weakness and vulnerability displayed by various colleagues that can be exploited if need be at a later date.

Divide and conquer

It is not uncommon for senior management, human resources managers, supervisors and co-workers to have different impressions of the same organisational psychopath. This is because the organisational psychopath has identified how useful each of these people can be, and for the 'chosen few' seen as useful, a specific impression is created.

Cultivating networks of power and influence

The level of power and influence a person has in the organisation is the most important evaluation criteria used by the psychopath. Senior managers, who often have very little to do with the organisational psychopath on a day-to-day basis, are charmed by this type of psychopath, and see them as a promising employee who needs to be looked after. The organisational psychopath will generally choose a specific target amongst senior management, doing similar activities (jogging, drinking after work, children at the same school, shopping, finishing and starting work at the same time) to allow frequent contact and eventual 'friendship'.

They will also try to charm the senior manager's personal assistant, giving them access to the senior manager at any time. The personal assistant also validates the senior manager's opinion of the organisational psychopath if ever he or she is asked. When this strategy is successful, the organisational psychopath has cleverly cultivated a very powerful ally in the organisation, who often tells the other senior managers about this 'promising employee'. Senior managers are usually intelligent people, who cannot afford to be wrong, particularly in front of their colleagues. Once their mind is made up it is difficult to change as senior managers are hesitant in recognising they have made a mistake about a person they thought they knew. It is only after repeated incidents are brought to their attention that they are forced to agree there 'may' be a problem, and establish a system to look into it.

Colleagues at the same level as the organisational psychopath are generally treated well while the psychopath settles in. They often report that the person was charming, fun to be with, made them feel good, intelligent, and was always there when needed. The psychopath appears to be everyone's friend, but in reality they are setting up their colleagues as 'unfavourable employees' to eliminate the competition when promotion time comes around. The first the victim knows of this 'back-stabbing' campaign is when they either complain about the psychopath (and are told the psychopath has already put in numerous complaints about them), or when they do not get the promotion they deserve. It is at this point that the psychopath's colleagues realise the true nature of their 'friend', but it is too late to do anything as the psychopath is usually senior to them and their complaints are often seen as malicious.

Colleagues junior to the psychopath are treated in a similar way. Generally they are conned into thinking the psychopath is their ally, until they become aware they have been used to further the psychopath's career, or simply for the psychopath's entertainment.

The mechanics of manipulation

The organisational psychopath typically goes through five stages when manipulating people on an individual level. These stages are intuitive for the psychopath rather than consciously used. However they are extremely powerful psychological techniques that effectively target a person's psychological vulnerability and then exploits that weakness for the psychopath's own ends.

Stage 1: Meeting the target

The organisational psychopath introduces themselves and bombards their victim with so much information that there is no time for their victim to think. Because the victim has no time to evaluate what the psychopath is saying, they are more likely to believe it. This is particularly true as the psychopath often throws in compliments that make the victim feel good about themselves. Therefore the victim likes being with the psychopath because they feel good about themselves and their lives, something they have usually not experienced in a long time. At this stage, the psychopath is friendly and appears willing do anything to please their victim.

Stage 2: Establishing rapport

The psychopath remains close to the victim, eliminating their ability to discuss the psychopath's behaviour with other people who are not emotionally involved in the situation. The psychopath maintains this rapport by continuing to discuss and participate in activities that interest the victim. The psychopath is making sure the victim's false perception of them is deeply ingrained.

Stage 3: Identify victim needs

The psychopath cleverly works out what the victim needs to hear so they can successfully con the victim. The psychopath identifies emotional weak points for the victim, such as not feeling loved, greed for more money, insecurity about financial future, desire to provide financial wealth for their family, desire for promotion, need to feel important in the organisation, wanting to feel included in the 'loop', and so on. Once a victim's need is identified, the psychopath tailors a set of lies that suggest or promise this need will be satisfied as long as the victim continues to trust the psychopath.

Stage 4: Create emotional pain

When the victim starts questioning and doubting the psychopath's promises, the behaviour changes. Still preying on the victim's emotional weak points, the psychopath now starts to attack them rather than boosting their self-esteem. They may threaten the victim, or imply that a person with already low self-esteem is 'stupid' for not trusting the psychopath, or ask how family members will feel when the victim does not get that promotion that is 'just around the corner'. They emphasise how the victim will feel if the emotional and physical dreams the psychopath has alluded to are not satisfied. For victims, the realisation that they have been conned by the psychopath is even more difficult to make; they have been encouraged to reflect on their dreams and believe they are about to come to fruition, only to have them shattered. This emotional torture is combined with the anguish of realising they have been used and then discarded.

Stage 5: Reverse psychology

The psychopath emphasises at this point that maybe the victim really does not deserve to have their desires fulfilled, as they do not have the courage or determination to achieve them with the psychopath's help. The victim, who trusted and often still does trust the psychopath, continues to do what the psychopath asks to prove their commitment to the psychopath. The psychopath often pretends that the victim has not done enough to regain their 'trust'. Often when the victim realises they have been conned their dignity suffers as well. They have very little confidence in their ability to make any decisions because trusting the organisational psychopath proved to be the biggest mistake of their lives.

Secrecy

Secrecy is fundamental to the survival of the organisational psychopath. To remain undetected they rely on each victim being unaware that other victims exist. If people who had been manipulated were to talk with each other about their experiences, the extent of the psychopath's deception would be revealed. Therefore the organisational psychopath is in a never-ending game of subterfuge, in which he or she uses social networks to spread misinformation so that no-one really knows the extent of the deceit.

It is this deliberate manipulation of social networks that sets the organisational psychopath apart from people who play office politics. When it comes to setting up and maintaining elaborate networks based on deceit the organisational psychopath is without peer. This is also one reason it is so difficult to deal with the organisational psychopath. One never knows who has been given misinformation in the organisation, and the psychopath makes sure people are too busy fighting for their own survival to worry about other possible victims. This is why knowledge and a tight group bond are the best defences against the organisational psychopath.

6

Effects on Victims

ONCE THE WORKPLACE psychopath has identified a victim, they use the strategies identified in previous chapters to 'hook' the unfortunate person. Whatever strategy the workplace psychopath uses against the victim, a number of similar responses are observed. Victims of the organisational psychopath characteristically report feeling as though they have lost control over their lives. Panic attacks, depression, disturbed sleep and nightmares, relationship problems, confusion, disbelief, guilt, lack of trust, anger, powerlessness, flashbacks, shame, embarrassment and sexual dysfunction are only some of the symptoms reported by victims.

Many victims who resign from their positions describe being unable to look for another job, as they do not trust people any more. Others lose all confidence in their capacity to perform adequately in their profession.

Employees who choose to stay frequently report feeling resentment toward a company to which they have given so much; they believe it has let them down by not believing or protecting them. Senior members of the company are also quite disillusioned when they discover that they have been manipulated by a psychopath.

What's happening to me?

People who have been physically, financially, psychologically or sexually victimised by a workplace psychopath have described experiencing a range of reactions and feelings, from shock and disbelief to anger and anxiety. While we all experience these sorts of feelings in the workplace at some stage in our working lives, it is the prolonged manipulation by a workplace psychopath to create these reactions that has a damaging effect. By learning to deal with these reactions in a positive way, the victim has a greater chance of surviving an encounter with a psychopath.

Shock and disbelief

When a person realises that they are being or have been manipulated or directly confronted by a psychopath, they can experience a sense of shock and disbelief, that 'it cannot be happening'. Some victims also say that they find it hard to accept that the confrontation or manipulation has happened, and feel that it must be them going crazy or imagining things, or blowing the situation out of proportion.

Mary's area manager sexually assaulted her while they were at a conference. He forced his way in to her room after a night of drinking and tried to kiss her. When Mary refused, he slapped her across the face and forced her to lie on the bed. Mary screamed and he ran from the room. Mary lay on her bed in absolute shock and terror that he would return. She then began to question whether it had really happened at all; it felt as though she were imagining the entire thing. When she went into the bathroom and saw the red marks on her face, she knew it was real. However, Mary did not report the area manager as he had a family and she did not want to break it up. She rationalised that he was drunk and was not really such a bad person; maybe she was exaggerating what had happened. Mary's area manager was later fired for sexually harassing a different victim.

Anger

Victims of workplace psychopaths may feel anger and hatred towards the psychopath for many different reasons. Anger is an emotion that people generally direct at others when they believe something bad or unfair is happening. This emotion usually goes hand-in-hand with a feeling of being threatened or unsafe. Sometimes this anger is not directed at the psychopath but towards someone close to the victim. This displaced anger happens when the victim cannot react or finds it difficult to get angry at the workplace psychopath.

Angry reactions can include impatience, acting on impulse, saying things that are regretted later, or becoming physically or verbally aggressive. Frequent anger reactions can become physically and emotionally draining, affect concentration and interfere with people's happiness and relationships. Long-term anger can affect the body's immune system, cause high blood pressure, increase the risk of heart disease and hypertension. It can also lead to alcohol or drug abuse as a form of self-medication to alleviate suffering being felt.

Feeling angry can often interfere with a person's ability to think rationally and clearly about the situation. The victim focuses on perceived violations and the injustices done to them by the psychopath, which can increase the feelings of anger. Victims often cannot stop thinking about the situation. Victims report mentally rehearsing every single detail of their exchange with the workplace psychopath, speculating about what may have happened 'if only' they had said or done something differently.

Some victims can become passive-aggressive. Passive-aggression is when a person tries to punish or hurt another person by using subtle strategies such as silence or withdrawing of attention. They may ignore or respond coldly to the psychopath and promise to do work they have no intention of completing. This sort of strategy generally exacerbates the situation for the victim.

Fear and anxiety

A feeling of apprehension and dread that something bad is going to happen is another response felt by a psychopath's victim. Characteristically these people fear other people, being in the presence of the psychopath, and the physical environment of their workplace.

Anxiety, like anger, is a state of physiological arousal that is often accompanied by unpleasant symptoms such as shortness of breath, sweaty palms, dry mouth, pounding heartbeat, muscle tension and tightness in the chest. Everyone feels anxious occasionally, it is a useful survival mechanism. However, continual feelings of anxiety that come from the person believing they can't escape the psychopath in their workplace becomes chronic anxiety. This is one of the most crippling psychological conditions as it stifles people's ability to enjoy life because they are always anxious and stressed.

Frank had been in the public service for nine years when he was promoted to a team leader position. He was extremely proud of his promotion, as he had studied at university at nights for the degree he needed to move up the public service ranks. He knew his duties inside out, and he was generally well liked by his peers.

Despite being prepared and working so hard to achieve his promotion, Frank was nervous on his first day in the new role. He met his team, and outlined what he expected of them. There was one team member who was extremely ambitious, and had also applied for the job that Frank won. He resented Frank's promotion and was determined to undermine him at every opportunity. He refused to do his job, ignored Frank (passive-aggression), deliberately made fun of Frank in front of the team, and openly said that Frank was not the person for the job. He also put in complaints about Frank to senior managers, fraudulently claiming that Frank did not have the support of the entire team.

Frank noticed that the other team members were losing respect for him, and some were openly defying him by not performing their duties.

Frank reported feeling tired all the time, constant tension headaches, lack of confidence in his ability, and on some occasions he even experienced panic-like reactions just prior to leaving for work. Frank was also irritable, and his wife reported more arguments since Frank's promotion. Frank constantly thought about work which made him even more anxious as he was reliving what happened each day.

Frank stayed in this position for two years before winning another promotion in a different department. When he moved, he noticed that his anxiety symptoms gradually disappeared within a few months.

Feeling anxious is not only a physical sensation. Anxiety also influences how victims think about their situation at work and at home. Feeling anxious can cause 'tunnel vision' that focuses victim attention on whatever is making them feel anxious. Tunnel vision limits the victim's ability to think clearly or to process other information in a normal way. For example, if a person is anxious about the behaviour of a workplace psychopath, they may plan to talk with the psychopath but then become so nervous that they cannot remember what they wanted to say. The person feels more helpless and their self-esteem plummets even lower.

While not all stress in the workplace is caused by the workplace psychopath, some signs of workplace stress include:

- Feeling irritable and/or tired
- Having trouble concentrating
- Loss of sense of humour
- More frequent arguments with those around you
- Lower productivity at work
- Sick more often
- Lack of concern about your work
- Attending work each day becomes an effort
- Loss of interest in activities outside of work

Shame and embarrassment

Some victims feel ashamed or embarrassed that they can't deal with a workplace psychopath. They also describe feeling as though everyone around them is aware of what is happening to them, and these people judge them as weak and useless. They often interpret what people say to them as relating to their specific experience and react inappropriately.

Jane was being victimised by an organisational psychopath in her position as a volunteer worker for a charity organisation. She was ashamed of what was happening to her, as she believed that she was a strong person who could look after herself. However, her self-esteem was spiralling downward as the psychopath relentlessly and systematically made her look bad in front of her co-workers. Jane was too ashamed to tell anyone what was happening to her at work.

She was out on a girls' night out when one of her friends commented that Jane should come out more often instead of doing so much volunteer work. To the surprise of her friends, Jane exploded, saying that no-one had the right to judge what she did with her time. She had mistakenly assumed that her friend was critical of how she 'let herself' be manipulated by the organisational psychopath. Her friend had no idea Jane was being manipulated; her innocent comment was misinterpreted by Jane because she was preoccupied and ashamed.

Feelings of shame and embarrassment can become so over-whelming that they impair a person's ability to function. Some victims refuse to interact with other people as they fear their 'secret' will be discovered. One client of mine, who had been victimised for many years, needed weekly reassurance that everything discussed in our counselling sessions was confidential. She believed that because she worked in an organisation that employed rich and powerful business people, her life would be destroyed if anyone found out that she had been victimised by one of them.

Fear of not being believed

Because psychopaths in the workplace are not recognised as a widespread problem, victims often report a fear that no-one will believe the terrible things that have been done to them. Often this fear of not being believed is reinforced when a manager or colleague does not believe the victim's allegations against the workplace psychopath. Fear of not being believed increases the sense of isolation, making them more vulnerable to the strategies used by the psychopath.

Sue had been living with a man who beat her repeatedly. He would treat her extremely badly, but he never left marks on her that could not be covered up by Sue's clothing. Sue kept her bruises covered because she was ashamed she 'let' the abuse happen. Everyone thought Sue's husband was fantastic, he was extremely charming in public and social situations. The neighbours thought he was great, Sue's family felt very fortunate that Sue had met such a nice man, and her husband's work colleagues enjoyed working with him.

When Sue finally reported what had been happening to the police, all of her 'friends' told her not to be foolish and make up things about her husband. That was until Sue showed them her bruises. It also turned out that Sue's husband had been embezzling money from his firm to cover gambling debts and expenses incurred from having a mistress who lived in a luxurious apartment and enjoyed first-class international travel. Some of her husband's colleagues still cannot believe it. They assumed a corporate and violent criminal psychopath would appear 'abnormal', not someone who was a trusted friend and colleague for many years.

Guilt and confusion

People often feel guilt about their inability to stand up to the workplace psychopath. They blame themselves for being manipulated or attacked. This self-blame and guilt can lead to confusion about the best course of action as the victim becomes caught up with anxiety trying to solve what seems like an unsolvable problem.

Feeling powerless, out of control or 'going crazy'

Victims of a workplace psychopath often feel there is a lack of control in their life. They find that their thoughts and behaviours are dominated by the workplace psychopath; constantly thinking about work and what they could have or should have done in certain situations. They have no control over when or how the psychopath is going to mistreat them. These people feel powerless and unable to change their situation.

The victim's interactions with other people often change as a result. This reinforces the feeling of being out of control because everything in their life appears to be changing, and it is negative or detrimental change. Life feels different for them. Once the victim thinks their life has changed, they often feel powerlessness because they cannot see any way of going back to their old life and feeling happy.

Lack of trust and a fear of people

The lack of trust of others is a direct result of the psychopath's continuous manipulation of the victim. The victim loses faith in other human beings as they have learned that people cause them emotional and sometimes physical pain. The fact that many victims initially liked and believed the psychopath when they first encountered them contributes to a loss of confidence in their ability to identify people who may be physically or psychologically dangerous.

Leanne was victimised so badly by an organisational psychopath that she was forced to leave a job that she initially loved. She attended numerous counselling sessions in which she developed strategies to find work and rebuild her self-esteem. Leanne eventually found a new job. The people she worked with were nice, but Leanne did not trust them. She openly documented everything they said and did in case she needed to use any of the information in future legal action. Her colleagues felt intimidated by this behaviour and did not interact with her. Leanne felt socially isolated and eventually quit her job. She believed that she was right not to trust anybody, as she did not actually get hurt when she was isolated by her colleagues. She had no insight that if she had opened herself up to them, she probably would have stayed in the job and regained some of her trust in other people.

Flashbacks

Victims often find that they keep replaying incidents where they were victimised by the psychopath. After a while, these constant thoughts may become flashbacks that are triggered by things that remind them of the incidents. For example, a particular smell, time of day, specific locations, or seeing someone who resembles the workplace psychopath. At first these flashbacks may be uncontrollable, but with time they generally become less frequent.

Sleep disturbances and nightmares

Disrupted sleeping patterns are another result of victim-isation. This can include an inability to get to sleep (insomnia), or oversleeping (hypersomnia). Nightmares can also be a common response although this usually settles down after some time has passed since the last incident experienced by the victim.

Relationship problems

Loss of trust in other people, a desire to be alone, a desire to be with someone all the time, and difficulties in intimate relationships are other outcomes from workplace victimisation. Because of the extreme effect on the victim, the workplace psychopath also has a negative impact on the victim's families and friends.

Depression

Everyone feels upset or sad from time to time, often triggered by disappointment or loss. Depression is a debilitating condition that interferes with a person's ability to experience pleasure, interact with other people, and participate in life. There are various degrees of sadness and depression, including a depressed mood, dysthymic disorder, and major or clinical depression.

Depressed mood is an emotional state that makes people feel sad, miserable, low and flat. Generally it passes after a short period of time. When a workplace psychopath is involved in causing depressed mood, this can become chronic and the depressed mood can last for long periods of time.

Dysthymic disorder is chronic mild depression. Victims feel constantly sad, pessimistic or generally apathetic. Other symptoms include low energy, low self-esteem, irritability, guilt, poor concentration, and difficulty making decisions. Victims often see themselves as uninteresting and incompetent, and become less involved in social situations.

Major depression is a more severe and disabling condition than dysthymic disorder. It includes low energy, loss of interest in things and a lack of pleasure. To be diagnosed with depression, five of the following characteristics (including at least one of the first two symptoms) should be experienced for at least a two-week period:

- Depressed mood for much of the day
- Reduced interest in pleasurable activities
- Changes in appetite or weight
- Changes in sleep patterns
- Lack of energy

- Feelings of guilt or worthlessness
- Agitation or slowing down of physical movements
- Inability to concentrate or make decisions
- Recurrent thoughts of death or suicide

Major depression can be mild, moderate or severe. People with mild depression are still able to function, though they experience little joy in doing so. People with moderate depression have greater social and occupational impairment. They may achieve little because of poor concentration or inability to relate to other people. People with severe depression experience a range of symptoms including changes in appetite, lack of energy, recurrent thoughts of death to name a few, and their ability to do anything at all is extremely limited. Even minor tasks such as getting out of bed or getting breakfast seem challenging to them.

Getting help

If you or someone you know is experiencing one or a number of these symptoms, it is important that professional assistance is sought. A number of different types of professionals can help. A psychiatrist, psychologist or counsellor can all help in different ways. It is important that the professional is well trained and experienced in dealing with issues that arise from contact with a workplace psychopath or other types of dysfunctional workplace behaviours.

Before getting help, it is useful for a victim to note what symptoms they are experiencing as a result of the workplace psychopath's treatment, such as:

- Anxiety, stress, excessive worry about your work situation
- Inability to sleep
- Racing heart
- Hyperventilation (fast, shallow breathing)
- Inability to concentrate
- Tension headaches or migraines
- Shame or embarrassment that result in a noticeable personality change
- Butterflies in the stomach while on the way to, going home from, or at work
- Aching or tired joints and muscles
- Depression
- Any skin complaints such as rashes, shingles, and so on that occur after the harassment started

- Abuse or overuse of substances such as alcohol, tobacco, prescription or illegal drugs to cope with the situation
- Hair loss
- High blood pressure
- Stomach ulcers
- Suicidal thoughts (you should see someone immediately if you are experiencing this)
- Chronic Fatigue Syndrome
- Glandular fever
- Significant weight loss or gain
- A feeling of exhaustion
- Feeling irritable or on edge all the time
- Difficulty trusting or believing in anybody
- Relationship problems (more fights, etc.)
- Loss of interest in sexual activity

It is also important for victims of the workplace psychopath not to feel as though they are experiencing the stress alone. Family and friends should be involved in the process if the victim feels comfortable with this, as they can provide very important support networks at a difficult time in the victim's life.

7

Protecting Yourself

HAVING AN ORGANISATIONAL psychopath in your life is physically, psychologically and emotionally draining. I receive numerous emails and letters from people saying that they have been victimised by a psychopath and pleading for a solution to make their situation 'go away'.

Unfortunately, there is no simple solution to managing the organisational psychopath. Strategies differ depending on the victim's work position in relation to the organisational psychopath. Strategies are also based on the characteristics of the individual psychopath and of the person being victimised. Victims are not always in a position that allows them to effectively manage an organisational psychopath.

Where an organisational psychopath can be managed, a number of general principles apply. Perhaps the most important of these come from research done by psychologists in human learning, organisational psychology, forensic psychology and clinical psychology.

The organisational psychopath as boss

If you have a boss who is an organisational psychopath, the damage they can do to your career begins before you are even aware there is a problem. We have seen that the organisational psychopath attacks on two fronts: they damage your reputation and they make your work environment an incredibly unpleasant (indeed, psychologically unhealthy) place to be.

Your boss can damage your reputation with upper management at meetings that you do not even know have occurred. Moreover, you probably are not invited to such meetings because they are 'above your pay grade'. Because upper management only know 'of you' based upon what your boss reports back to them, they may have an extremely negative impression of you without you knowing that there is a problem. The only effective way to counter this strategy deployed is to make sure that there is no basis for unfair allegations to be made against you. It is equally important to ensure that upper management are aware enough of your work to realise that you are a valuable employee.

Sue worked as a mid-level public servant for a government agency. She came to see me because she could not take the stress of work any longer. Her boss was making life at work so hard that she cried at night and feared going to work each day. Sue felt completely hopeless about the situation; when she had made a report about how her boss treated her, she had been told that she was about to be placed on a performance management program as her boss felt she was a problem employee. Upper management said they had been fully briefed by her boss over the last few months about her work performance and that her complaint appeared to be an attempt to discredit her boss's poor reviews. Upper management agreed to look into Sue's complaint but she heard nothing from them subsequently. Sue was in an extremely difficult situation, which, for her own wellbeing, clearly had to change. Ultimately, Sue found a new job and then resigned from her old one. She did it in this order so that her boss could not sabotage her

efforts to secure a new job. This was the first time in the
situation that Sue took control and it resulted in a successful
outcome for her.

To 'victim-proof' yourself, it is important to implement your
strategies right from the beginning of your employment. The
first step is to make sure you are known to upper management. Be prepared to chat to them about your work and the
company when you encounter them, and make sure they
know of your role in major projects that are a success for the
organisation. You need to manage your colleagues' impressions of you to ensure that their impressions accurately reflect
the good work you are doing.

The organisational psychopath talks to upper management,
ingratiates themselves with key players in the organisation and
makes it known that they are doing good work (even when
that good work was done by someone else). The difference
between the organisational psychopath and you is that they are
managing impressions to manipulate people and cover for
their poor performance, while you are doing it for honest
reasons. Although the reasons differ, the process is very similar.

You should also document everything that happens to you
if you have a psychopathic boss. Make a note of it in your

diary, and if there are witnesses, have them sign it as well. Keep your notes brief and to the point, and only include factual behaviours. Leave out your personal opinions of the boss and the situation. It is a legal document, not your thoughts about another person. This means that you do not call them a psychopath. First, you are not qualified to make such a judgement, and second, it may appear unprofessional and reduce the credibility of your claims.

When your boss assigns you a task, make sure that you clarify all aspects of that task with him or her in writing (for example, via email). Again, be very concise: outline the resources allocated to you, a timeframe, and what you are expected to deliver. This is to ensure that the organisational psychopath cannot claim to have given you a different task when trying to damage your credibility. You should have the organisational psychopath confirm everything in writing if possible (by replying to your email). However, not all organisational psychopaths will respond as they do not want to lock themselves into a scenario if they need to lie about it later. To get around this, you need to email them as described above, but a phrase like 'unless I am instructed differently'. You could even include a statement at the end of your email that no reply is indicative of agreement. A number of organisations view this practice as a little 'different' at first, but they come to appreciate it as a very professional because you are trying to clarify the objectives and performance outcomes of your task.

As well as documenting tasks, make sure to document incidents in writing. This is what human resources staff will ask you for if you have to make a complaint. They will want evidence of actual behaviours, not speculative opinions from you about what is occurring.

Try not to complain about your boss in a negative manner; no-one likes unconstructive complaints that sound like personal attacks. For example, instead of saying 'Tom was very rude to me in the office yesterday – he lost his temper and called me a ?#$@!#', you could say something like 'I am really worried about Tom – he swore at me yesterday and I do not understand why. I was asking him to clarify task ABC when suddenly he flew off the handle'. Both statements get your point across, however one is more of a personal attack than the other.

You need to act in a professional manner at all times when dealing with a psychopathic boss. Never engage in shouting matches, never call them a psychopath, and do not try to spread rumours about them. If you do so, your own credibility will be damaged, sometimes beyond repair, and you are playing right into the hands of the psychopath. Besides, when it comes to playing these sorts of games an experienced workplace psychopath is likely to be far better at it than you. If you hear rumours that are untrue, you need to correct them immediately (whether they are about you or someone else) to minimise the damage they can cause.

You need to understand where you stand in the organisation. Do you have the support of the HR department and upper management if you make a complaint? Will you be given a negative reference (or none at all) if you leave? Have you complained every Monday for the past year about your boss with no result? Are you seen as a serial complainer rather than as a victim with a legitimate problem?

Once you have evaluated the power differential between you and the organisational psychopath, you should calculate the costs and benefits of staying and of leaving your organisation or department. It may be better for you to accept a position in a different department within the same organisation to retain your benefits. Or it may be wiser for you to find a job with a different organisation. It is much better for you to try to find a solution well before it comes to the point where you are forced to leave (either by the organisation or for mental health reasons). Your boss may even surprise you and give you a good recommendation to get rid of you. Workplace psychopaths will follow the 'path of least resistance', and if that means saying what it takes to get you a transfer or a new job, that is what they will do. However, you should set in place the framework and support network for finding a different role well before your psychopathic boss knows you are even thinking about transferring. The less they know, the less information they can use to damage you.

The organisational psychopath as co-worker

If a person you work with is really an organisational psychopath, you should realise that they do not care about you at all. They are quite prepared to use you to complete their work, and to damage your reputation because it makes them look good. They absolutely cannot be trusted, and you should try to keep as much distance between you and the psychopath as possible.

For anyone working at the same level as an organisational psychopath, self-protection guidelines are similar to those for dealing with a psychopathic boss. Make sure to note everything in writing, be professional, make sure you have a good network of people (at all levels of your organisation) who know that you do good work, and do not try to compete with the psychopath at their own game. Confronting or trying to manipulate the psychopath carries an extremely high risk of disaster. You should also evaluate the costs and the benefits of leaving or transferring to another workplace.

In addition to these general principles, there are a number of specific strategies for dealing with a psychopathic colleague. Most importantly, you should never cover for or finish the organisational psychopath's work for them. This 'covering' behaviour can easily be used against you, as the psychopath is expert at blaming you for not completing their work and making it appear as though their task was actually yours.

You should consider officially reporting their behaviour; it is likely that they are manipulating other people you work with as well. Communicating with colleagues about what is happening to you reduces your sense of isolation. However, such communication should be done in a professional manner that cannot be viewed as 'office politics' or 'ganging up' on the psychopath. Remember, the psychopath will have people in the organisation who will protect them, so this strategy should be used with caution. Understand the potential consequences for yourself if you make a report about the person.

The organisational psychopath as employee

The psychopathic subordinate is a significant challenge for any manager; they have the potential to destroy a manager's career. It is only when the organisational psychopath is universally accepted by the organisation as a problem that a coherent, well-defined management solution can be implemented successfully.

Even if the organisational psychopath is recognised as a problem (and this does not always occur by any means), handling them is a difficult proposition at best because they do not want 'help' to improve their behaviour. For them, life and work are all about self-gratification. Rather than try to change, the organisational psychopath will pretend they *have* changed, all the while trying to damage their boss professionally any way they can.

The manager of an organisational psychopath should also implement the common 'defensive strategies': communicate with upper management, act professionally, make written notes of everything, and ensure that channels of communication with all co-workers are open and honest. There are some other general principles that a manager can use to deal with an organisational psychopath, as well as specific day-to-day techniques.

General psychopath management

If an organisation recognises they have an organisational psychopath working for them, and if they are committed to dealing with this, certain management strategies can be put in place. These strategies are based upon what are called instrumental learning principles. Instrumental learning is a form of learning based on reinforcing (positively or negatively) and/or punishing behaviours that are either desirable or undesirable. The first and most important aspect of instrumental learning is the 'law of effect'. This law governs whether a behaviour will be repeated or eliminated from a person's repertoire. It states that the consequences of a behaviour determine whether the behaviour is likely to be repeated. In other words, future behaviour patterns are shaped by rewarding or punishing existing behaviour patterns. Three different types of instrumental learning strategies exist: positive reinforcement, negative reinforcement and punishment. Any or all of these can be used to manage an organisational psychopath.

Positive reinforcement is where a behaviour is rewarded with something that appeals to the person whose behaviour is in question. For example, a child is rewarded with an ice-cream after cleaning his or her room. This means that in future it is more likely that the child will clean his or her room as this is associated with getting an ice-cream. This positive reinforcement also applies to the organisational psychopath, who is motivated by self-gratification. For example, the organisational psychopath will do whatever it takes to make a sale to receive a commission. In the long term making a large number of sales may be followed by a promotion which brings an increase in power over other people in the organisation.

It is very important when managing the psychopath to examine what behaviours the organisational psychopath has previously been rewarded for. Have they been promoted for being ruthless, manipulative and lying? It is common for this to occur. The corporation may have been encouraging the psychopath's behaviour by rewarding it.

Negative reinforcement is where a behaviour is followed by the termination of an unpleasant event. There are two types of learning associated with negative reinforcement: *avoidance learning* and *escape learning*. Avoidance learning occurs when a person prevents an expected negative event from happening, such as putting on sunscreen before going to the beach to stop the negative event of getting sunburned. An organisational psychopath in sales may learn to avoid negative events such as a reduction in their commission for dishonest behaviour by telling the truth about a product and ensuring clients are satisfied.

Jenny is an organisational psychopath who averages $100,000 in sales per month. She consistently makes the most sales in her section, and works on a commission basis of 10 per cent. Jenny also has the highest number of dissatisfied customers, most of whom claim that Jenny lied about what the product was capable of doing. Many of these customers want to return their products, which has the potential of costing the company financially as well as affecting their reputation. A simple learning strategy was put in place to shape Jenny's behaviour.

Jenny was told that for every dissatisfied customer the company determined had been deceived, she would lose $1500 for the sale – $1000 commission and $500 to reimburse the company for expenses. Jenny quickly learned that if she was honest with her customers, and still used her charm to sell products, she was able to average seven sales per month, making $7000. If she lied to customers, she had an average of four customers return their products, which meant that Jenny only made $4000 per month on average after being charged $6000 (four lots of $1500 in penalties) from the total commission of $10,000. It was more financially rewarding for her to be honest about the products she was selling. Jenny avoided the negative event of losing money by being honest with her clients.

Escape learning is a term used to describe how a person learns to escape a situation in order to avoid a negative experience. For example, imagine a noisy air-conditioner continually disturbs someone who is trying to sleep. One evening, they get out of bed and kick the air-conditioner, stopping the noise. The next time the air-conditioner makes a noise, they are likely to kick it because in their mind kicking it causes the noise to stop. In other words, they have learned that behaviour (kicking) stops a negative experience (being disturbed by a noisy air-conditioner). In the case of the organisational psychopath, the unpleasant event of being constantly monitored and placed on probation for bullying is terminated when they change their behaviour and stop bullying co-workers. They learn that termination of an unpleasant event (being on probation and constantly monitored) is associated with stopping their bullying behaviour.

When trying to change a person's negative behaviour, particularly the organisational psychopath, punishment is instinctively the most obvious approach. However, punishment is different to positive/negative reinforcement because it is less effective in shaping or changing a person's behaviour. Punishment can involve a negative consequence for a behaviour, such as a child being spanked for swearing. In the case of the organisational psychopath, they may be fined each time they are found to be taking credit for work done by a colleague. Punishment can also involve the removal of a reward when a person does an unfavourable behaviour. For example, an organisational psychopath could be demoted from an 'acting management' role as a result of behaviour that is seen as undesirable by their employer.

One learning approach that has proved to be successful in the management of the organisational psychopath is the use of a system known as the 'token economy'. Token economies work on reinforcing appropriate behaviour while simultaneously punishing undesirable behaviour through the use of 'tokens' or rewards that 'buy' certain things. How this works on the organisational psychopath's behaviour is quite simple. Knowing that an organisational psychopath desires power and influence (promotion) and financial rewards (pay increases) can be used as a reward system – like an old-fashioned gold star chart. Tokens or reward points are earned by the psychopath for behaviour that appeals to them (for example, large sales equals big commission) and also works to the benefit of others (favourable ratings by staff, good customer feedback, and so on). Reward points are deducted for behaviours such as staff complaints, bullying co-workers, failing to attend meetings, etc. The criteria for awarding or deducting points is set by the organisation based on what they feel is important to the company. The psychopath is told that under a performance management scheme they will be promoted and/or receive a pay increase (or other goals that would gratify the psychopath) when they get a certain number of reward points.

Because the psychopath is easily bored and lacks motivation for long-term planning, short-term benefits for achieving a certain number of 'reward points', such as days off work, movie tickets, golf days, is a good thing to implement. Other employees should also be able to earn similar rewards for good work so that they do not see the psychopath being treated as 'special' by the organisation.

A learning-based management program does not change the fact that the employee is an organisational psychopath. Instead, it seeks to reduce staff distress, increase productivity, decrease client dissatisfaction, and reduce staff turnover rates by managing the organisational psychopath's behaviour.

Day-to-day management strategies

There are also a number of specific day-to-day management tactics that can be used in conjunction with a psychopath management plan.

In addition to planned meetings, visit the psychopath in their office/workspace unannounced. This creates the feeling that they are being monitored and makes them less inclined to flagrantly disregard the rules.

If the organisational psychopath insists on meeting with you repeatedly simply to inconvenience you, schedule these meetings for just before the psychopath wants to go home. If this does not seem to affect the psychopath, try and make sure that the meetings run well beyond the organisational psychopath's scheduled finish time.

Plan management sessions very carefully. Understand the objectives of the session, and make sure that these objectives are addressed specifically and succinctly. Have the organisational psychopath commit to the goals of the management program in writing so they are unable to later claim ignorance. Think about possible rebuttals from the workplace psychopath to points in the management plan and have answers ready to counter them.

If the organisational psychopath appears to become 'emotional' during a meeting, wait for them to calm down. If this does not happen, reschedule the meeting. If they use the 'emotional' tactic again, address the management criteria in writing, verifying that they have received the written document and requesting a response within a very specific time frame. Emphasise that if they do not respond, obviously they do not take the company seriously and it may be appropriate for them to seek employment elsewhere.

Do not allow the organisational psychopath to sidetrack the management discussion. Have a written list of points to be addressed and do not deviate from these points for any reason. It is almost certain that the psychopath will attempt to sidetrack the discussion to prevent being restricted by the management criteria.

If the organisational psychopath arrives late to work or takes days off after the management meeting, make sure they are instructed in writing to ring you and explain why they are absent each time. Record these answers and compare them from day to day for consistency. Also watch for patterns in these absences (for example, Mondays and Fridays).

If you hear rumours that you know are untrue, immediately correct them with the truth. It is important to take prompt action, as this will minimise the damage caused by the organisational psychopath's rumours.

Document everything in writing. This will ensure that the psychopath cannot escape responsibility for his or her behaviours.

If you are deliberately blamed for not producing work by the workplace psychopath, particularly after implementing or discussing the management strategy, there are a number of options available. Always document the accusation, and ask for the complaint in writing.

If you are a team leader, make sure that you have the support of your team. If you don't it is possible the psychopath will turn your team against you and undermine the management strategy you are trying to put in place.

When the management strategy is implemented, you should expect the organisational psychopath to play office politics harder than ever before as they attempt to avoid the conditions imposed by the management strategy. There are a number of things you can do to minimise the impact of these political games. If you are a supervisor or manager, discourage workers who attempt to win your favour over other workers, as this can build resentment. However, it is important not to alienate your employees at the same time. Avoid being seen to have personal friendships with subordinates. Make sure that people who play office politics are given enough work to do, and monitor work performance to minimise their time to do 'non-work' related activities.

Know where the power lies in your organisation, so that you can consult these people in case the politics get out of control. Always be courteous and friendly with everyone, and never neglect your own office politics self-defence strategy.

Know yourself

No matter whether you are a manager, colleague, or employee of a psychopath, you can also minimise your risk of being victimised by developing a greater awareness of your own psychological make-up and vulnerabilities. The psychopath plays on these vulnerabilities, and if you recognise what they are doing you can circumvent their manipulative strategies from the outset.

8

Inoculating Employees

PROTECTING EMPLOYEES FROM the workplace psychopath can be done on a group and an individual level. Group protection involves educating employees about the characteristics of the workplace psychopath to minimise their chances of being victimised. Team-building exercises are helpful in eliminating the psychopath's ability to isolate individual team members. At an individual level, by addressing self-confidence and self-esteem issues through life-coaching programs and stress management techniques, each employee's vulnerability to a psychopath's assault is lessened. Both group and individual protection strategies need to be specifically tailored depending upon the exact nature of the workplace psychopath.

Employee education

The best way to start dealing with this problem is to talk to employees in general terms about bullying in the workplace. The characteristics of workplace psychopaths can then be elaborated upon in the context of addressing bullying. Discretion is critical when educating employees about the potential threats within their workplace.

It is not necessary to refer to or use the word 'psychopath' at all in these types of education strategies, as the word 'psychopath' conjures images of serial killers and other criminals that cloud the reality of the workplace situation. What is particularly important is that employees recognise the person's behaviour as inappropriate, not whether they can label it as 'psychopathic' or not. The case study below provides an example of one approach to this education and team building strategy.

> I was asked by a call centre to assess why a significant number of staff were resigning from one particular team. Traditionally the call centre industry has a high staff turnover rate as it is, but in this particular section 70 per cent of staff had resigned in a two-month period. Importantly, the high staff resignation rate coincided with the appointment of Jenny, a new team leader.

After a detailed assessment and psychological profile was completed, I determined that Jenny displayed many behaviours and traits that were characteristic of the organisational psychopath.

I advised the company that the best approach would be to commence an education campaign and team-building exercises to combat the techniques used by this particular organisational psychopath. The education campaign was implemented in conjunction with a strategy that used learning principles to manage Jenny's behaviour.

All team members and team leaders in the call centre (including Jenny) were educated at a staff training day about various types of bullying behaviour and its effects on employees. The personality and behavioural characteristics of the organisational psychopath were also outlined in the context of explaining why certain types of bullying behaviour occur. Moreover, the tactics and strategies used by the organisational psychopath were discussed. This ensured that people recognised what was occurring when Jenny manipulated situations, allowing them to recognise and manage her behaviour.

A separate team-building day was held specifically for Jenny's team. This training did not include Jenny. It was explained to her that the team members needed to work together, and sometimes the presence of the team leader had a negative effect on this development process. After the team-building exercises, each team member reported feeling better about their work and their situation. They also reported feeling more comfortable about working with Jenny as they had a network of colleagues they could freely talk to about any problems they were having.

On an individual level, team members were educated about the physiology and psychology of stress, depression and anger. They were also shown how to reduce stress in their lives through some simple stress-management techniques. The call-centre industry is stressful by nature, and the exercises they learned were rated as highly useful not only to cope with Jenny, but also when they were feeling 'burnout' associated with other aspects of their work environment.

Finally, an individual life coaching program was developed with each team member. This coaching program looked at challenging negative or limiting thought patterns, setting realistic and achievable goals, and recognising psychological vulnerabilities that could be played upon by the organisational psychopath.

When the entire intervention program was evaluated after three months, no staff members had resigned, and each reported feeling happier and more in control of their workplace and themselves. None of the team members liked working with

Jenny, but they felt they could cope with her behaviours and prevent her from manipulating them or other team members. Their productivity increased, and most important of all they felt valued and believed by the organisation they worked for because senior management had noticed and taken action about dissatisfaction in their section.

Staff education is important because it addresses and eliminates the distressing reactions victims face when dealing with the workplace psychopath. Crucial to strengthening how staff and individuals deal with the psychopath is getting rid of the 'blame' factor where people blame themselves for the destructive behaviour that happens.

Education creates an awareness of the existence and reality of the workplace psychopath. This means that the problem is external to the victim and is not seen by them as being their fault.

Team building

The organisational psychopath often exploits existing conflicts between employees, or they will create new ones. They play on the fact that employees tend to work independently, are often self-focused and have hidden agendas concerning their work, may distrust other team members, have disagreements that are not constructive, and they often do not have clear channels of communication. These factors can create conflict and peer pressure to conform with the majority of the group.

A good team-building strategy can encourage inter-dependence between team members as well as openness and trust. Disagreements are seen as positive and constructive parts of the change process rather than competitions for power between team members. Honest and transparent communication should be encouraged, which then allows for free expression rather than conformity to group expectations. Importantly, conflict resolution procedures need to be set in place so that team members become a unified group rather than a set of independent people. It is this unity that protects employees from the organisational psychopath.

If a consultant is called in, it is important for them to be familiar with the reason for the team-building exercise. Also, it is preferable that they have some knowledge of how the workplace psychopath can effect other employees.

The consultant meets with the human resources and senior management sections in the organisation. The relevance and usefulness of team building is evaluated, and organisational goals are defined. These goals can include increased productivity, reduced sick days, and protection from the workplace psychopath. Employees should also be allocated to specific teams at this stage of the team-building process. Administrative and evaluation criteria should be established to make sure there is no confusion later. For example, frequency and location of team meetings, performance indicators, feedback procedures, and so on, should all be discussed.

The consultant meets and establishes rapport with individual team members. The consultant should acknowledge team members' concerns, uncertainty about the process, and encourage open expression of ideas. Expectations for each team member are also clarified so that each team member knows what is expected of him or her.

Team members meet as a 'team' for the first time. Team members discuss their needs and wants, and the consultant addresses organisational needs. Issues such as why the team has been formed, goals of the team, and the importance of a unified approach are all discussed in an open forum. If team members have not worked together before, a team building exercise is useful. This 'exercise' may range from solving hypothetical problems in the office to a week-long retreat in the wilderness or learning to scuba dive together. It is important that team members develop trust in one another, and know they can count on each other for support in difficult situations.

A second team meeting is organised after the 'bonding exercise'. Group goals are solidified, team members' questions are clarified, and any resistance from individual team members to the overall goals is explored.

Ongoing meetings with the team take place where progress is discussed. The reaction of the workplace psychopath to the unified team is also dealt with. Feedback is provided to team members, and the human resources department and senior managers are given feedback about the performance of the team in relation to the workplace psychopath's manipulative strategies.

Employee life coaching and self-esteem maintenance

Life coaching and a self-esteem maintenance program are valuable tools that can be used to protect individual employees from the psychopath's destructive influence. Both of these strategies counteract the effects of the psychopath's attempts to isolate and degrade their victim, as they work on encouraging the victim to take active control of their lives and to see themselves as valuable.

Life coaching programs get employees to look closely at their values, perception of themselves and set goals to enrich their lives. Life coaching encourages the individual to focus on defining personal goals and then working towards achieving them. This moves the person away from focusing on fixing negatives (such as a workplace psychopath) while restoring a belief in themselves and taking control of their lives back.

Life coaching also looks at obstacles that prevent an individual from achieving goals. These obstacles can include fear of the unknown, fear of failure, fear of disapproval and fear of making the wrong decision. Other obstacles to making meaningful and lasting change in response to a workplace psychopath are financial limitations, low self-esteem, lack of decisiveness, habit, lack of skills necessary to make a change, lack of energy, and the needs of other people in a victim's life conflicting with their own needs. A life coach can help the victim to overcome these obstacles by showing a person how to implement a series of smaller, more manageable goals that gradually lead to a more positive change. However, life coaching is only an effective strategy when the organisational psychopath is managed by the organisation. Life coaching is not 'the' solution, it is part of an overall strategy to deal with workplace psychopaths.

Teaching employees about self-esteem maintenance is also a useful strategy because it reduces the victim's vulnerability to the workplace psychopath's tactics. Healthy self-esteem comes from self-acceptance, rather than relying on what other people think of us. This means accepting flaws and perceived imperfections, without believing that these imperfections make us worthless. Moreover, when dealing with the workplace psychopath, it is important to accept that not everyone will approve of or like us. It is also important to challenge negative statements based upon what the victim knows about themself.

One useful approach for psychologically challenging the workplace psychopath's claims is Cognitive Behavioural Therapy, which encourages people to look at the feelings caused by a particular situation. These feelings are looked at closely to identify and recognise the thoughts and beliefs that create these feelings. Any beliefs or thoughts that don't contribute to feeling positive are then questioned. After disputing these unhelpful beliefs, positive action is taken so that these negative beliefs do not affect the quality of one's life. For example:

- *Situation* – Jane has been told by her boss (who is an organisational psychopath) that she is a useless employee and he cannot understand how she was given her job in the first place.
- *Feelings* – Jane feels worthless, she cannot do anything right at work.
- *Thoughts* – My boss thinks I am useless; he hates me; he wishes he did not have to see me every day.
- *Beliefs* – Because I cannot please my boss I am worthless, useless. I should be liked by my boss. My boss should be happy with my work.
- *Dispute* – I am highly qualified and experienced in my job. I have never had a problem before. I have won awards for my excellent performance in the past. Just because this boss tells me I cannot do my job, does not mean I am useless or worthless. Some people like my work and others don't. People are all different. My boss and I have different expectations about what is 'good work' and that is okay.
- *Positive actions* – Stop focusing on what my boss thinks of me and my work. Relax and focus on getting the job done to a standard that I know is good.

Stress management

Employees are invariably placed under a great deal of stress when they share a workplace with the psychopath. Stress management techniques can be taught to reduce and help manage levels of stress. Like life coaching these techniques are not a complete 'solution' to the workplace psychopath.

There are a number of things that can be done to help reduce stress levels and to create a 'stress resilience'. This includes moderating your physical reactions to stress through relaxation techniques, deep breathing, meditation; building on your physical reserves through regular exercise, a healthy balanced diet and getting plenty of sleep; maintaining your emotional reserves such as managing your time, developing a strong support network of friends and family. Stress management techniques are many and varied. Consult with a psychiatrist, psychologist or a counsellor to find out about techniques that are suitable for the situation.

Should I stay or resign?

It is important to note that once a person realises a workplace psychopath is not able to be controlled or managed easily without the support of their organisation, the best strategy for them is often to leave the workplace and find a new job. It has been recognised in psychology for some time that a stressor (such as a workplace psychopath) that is external to the self and cannot be controlled or predicted poses the greatest psychological danger to a person. I have seen numerous victims who have decided to stay with their employer as a matter of principle, for financial reasons, because they have invested X number of years in the company, because they feel likethey could not get another job, etc. These victims are often severely psychologically traumatised.

This is not to say that everyone who encounters a workplace psychopath and has their complaint ignored by an organisation should leave their position. The important question to ask is: 'At what point does a person's psychological and physical health become more important than their job?'

It may not be fair that a person has to leave their job on account of a workplace psychopath making their life unbearable. Unfortunately, the expectation that life should be fair does not match what happens in the real world. For example, is it fair that people born in poor families have higher death rates and less opportunities than children born in wealthy families? Is it fair that in many workplaces you can find talented employees being poorly rewarded for working hard while others in senior positions may lack competence yet be paid significantly more? Even though people may wish the world was always fair, it is not. It is possible to spend a great deal of energy and time dwelling on how unfair the situation is, as opposed to telling oneself that life can be unfair and that it is necessary to move on and find a different place to work.

The ethics of labelling

The workplace psychopath is usually reluctant to be a part of the consulting process. However, it is typical for a consultant to be engaged by the organisation because they have a responsibility to their employees and clients to minimise harm once a problem employee is identified. Therefore the consultant's primary responsibility is to the organisation rather than the specific employee. This is not to say that the psychopath and colleagues of the psychopath do not have rights, just that they must be carefully balanced with the desire of the organisation to eliminate the damage being caused by the psychopath. This is similar to an organisational psychologist who specialises in recruitment testing having a primary responsibility to the organisation employing them, but an additional, secondary responsibility, to the people they are testing on behalf of the organisation.

On most occasions the organisation is not in a position to determine whether the 'problem employee' is in fact a psychopath. Therefore it is imperative that a qualified consultant is employed who can identify the cause of the problem, rather than simply developing a solution that may be based upon an inaccurate diagnosis of 'psychopathy' made by a person in the organisation who is not qualified or experienced enough to make such a diagnosis. Hence the first ethical responsibility for any consultant when managing an organisational psychopath is to establish a valid diagnosis of the problem.

Once a diagnosis is made, the consultant must then advise the organisation whether the best course of action is to dismiss the psychopath from their job, or implement a management strategy to keep the psychopath's behaviours in check. There is no simple rule used to make this determination, it can only be decided on a case by case basis. However, a careful balance needs to be achieved between the needs of the organisation, the workplace psychopath and all employees.

There are a number of strategies that can be used to limit the damaging effect a workplace psychopath can have on individuals and organisations. These strategies don't stand alone, however, and need to be integrated with different coping and prevention techniques for them to be effective.

Treatment can make them worse

There is no effective treatment for psychopathy because it is a pervasive personality disorder that has taken many years to form. A fundamental assumption of any therapy program is that the person seeking treatment wants help, and is willing to change their behaviours. The psychopath does not seek help because they view their self-gratifying behaviours as fulfilling their needs. In *Without Conscience*, Dr Hare states that 'psychopaths don't feel they have psychological or emotional problems, and they see no reason to change their behaviour to conform to societal standards with which they do not agree ... they see themselves as superior beings in a hostile, dog eat dog world in which others are competitors for power and resources' (p. 195).

9

Good for Business?

CAN A WORKPLACE psychopath be of benefit to the company they work for? Is it possible for a person with no conscience or remorse to use their personality characteristics to make more money for themselves and/or their employer? At what human cost does this profit come?

The answers to these questions are complex. Each answer depends on a number of factors, including what industry the psychopath is working in and who is evaluating the value of the psychopath. A shareholder will provide a different answer to a CEO, who will provide a different answer again to a customer or the person who has to work with the workplace psychopath.

The simple answer to whether a psychopath can be useful to a company is no. In the short term they can generate sales with their verbal abilities, or persuade people in the company to take new directions, but in the long term the company will usually suffer. This is because the psychopath, regardless of profession, is concerned with only one thing – self-gratification. This self-gratification is obtained irrespective of the cost to people around them, or to the company they work for. Unless the psychopath's self-interest is the same as that of the company, the company will ultimately lose. Moreover, even if the psychopath and the company share similar goals, the psychopath often alienates and exploits co-workers to achieve this goal. This can result in the loss of valued, highly trained staff, which ultimately comes out of the company bottom-line.

The financial cost does not even begin to account for the psychological damage caused to co-workers.

What is 'good for business'?

Corporations generally measure their success in terms of how much money they make, while government agencies critique how effectively they perform their legislated responsibilities. Employees are viewed as a means to an end, resources used to make money or enforce legislation.

Therefore 'good for business' would be defined by the decision-makers in big business and government as the amount of profit made each year, or the number of times and effectiveness with which legislation is enforced. Secondary considerations include employee welfare, staff retention rates, sick leave taken by each employee, training costs, and human resources and recruitment costs. Each of these secondary considerations is emphasised because they can affect the productivity of staff, and therefore the amount of profit made or quality of services delivered.

In recent years, corporations began to realise that the better they treated their employees, the more productivity they observed for each worker. This philosophy is still reflected in the development of numerous workplace programs designed to make employees feel a part of the 'corporate culture', to reduce stress in the workplace, to emphasise that they are valued employees, etc. It is important to note that the success of these programs is measured in terms of increases in productivity or decreases in costs such as sick leave and employee resignations.

Society's view of what is 'good for business' does not necessarily take into account employee welfare unless this issue is affecting profits. This approach is not motivated by sinister forces that control and exploit workers for the sake of a few wealthy people in society. It is simply a product of living in a capitalist economy whereby society revolves around the exchange of goods and services for money. The vast majority of businesses are started with the aim of making money. Large businesses are usually accountable to shareholders, who are only concerned with how much profit the company makes each year as this affects how much money they will receive as a dividend, as well as the value of their stocks. The directors of the company are employed on the understanding that they will endeavour to make the largest possible profit each year for the company. Therefore employees are seen as a resource needed to provide goods and services that can be exchanged for money. If the employees function well together, the company makes more money. From this perspective, the workplace psychopath is evaluated in terms of how much additional income they can contribute to the company.

From a government agency perspective, the psychopath is evaluated in terms of how well they achieve the agency goals, whatever these may be. Government agencies generally focus on productivity, employee welfare is covered under the award agreements, but it is not necessarily a priority to provide working conditions that exceed those defined by the award.

I would argue that as a society, it is also important to measure success in both business and government agencies in terms of balancing the human cost with profitability and service provision. Unfortunately, it is often the case that providing better working conditions for employees impacts on profitability or service provision, and therefore the human cost becomes a secondary issue.

Profit-maker or liability?

At first glance, the organisational psychopath may appear to have significant contributions they can make to a company. They possess good verbal skills, are experienced at manipulating people, are prepared to do whatever it takes to achieve their goals, and they may be creative as a result of their being prone to boredom leading to the development of new ideas. In the short term, these attributes may lead to increased revenue. However, this positive contribution can be misleading.

In the short term, the organisational psychopath may generate sales, or embark on ambitious projects that promise to make the firm large sums of money. The customer is happy as they have been promised big things and the company is happy as they look forward to receiving additional income. However, as we have already seen, the organisational psychopath will not hesitate to lie about what they can deliver. In addition, they are not prepared to actually do the work required, making up excuses for why it is not completed and blaming everyone other than themselves. This causes the customer to become very dissatisfied in the long term, and they cancel the contract. From a Customer Relationship Management perspective, the customer will not be returning to do business with the company again. Worse, they tell other companies about their bad experience with the psychopath and the company they work for, creating negativity and uncertainty about the company who did not deliver as promised. This company then has to advertise not only their product, but they also have to convince people that they are reliable and can deliver goods or services as promised. The value of this damage caused by the psychopath cannot be calculated. What is the cost to a company of losing their reputation? In some cases it can be bankruptcy.

So in the short term the organisational psychopath may generate additional profit, but in the long term the company loses as their reputation has been damaged, sometimes beyond repair. From a profit perspective, the organisational psychopath is not desirable.

The human cost of employing an organisational psychopath in a company can be astronomical, both financially for the company and psychologically for the victims. The financial cost to the company often easily exceeds the profit the psycho-path makes for the company in the initial stages of their employment. Staff resigning, recruitment costs, training costs for new staff, and legal actions taken against the company all add up to substantial amounts of money. Authors Helene Richards and Sheila Freeman in *Bullying in the Workplace: An Occupational Hazard* estimate that in Australia $36 billion is lost due to damages payouts to former employees and loss of productivity as a result of bullying. Perhaps more importantly, organisational psychopaths take away from time that the com-pany could be using to generate additional business or expand relationships held with current customers.

Psychologically for other staff members, lives are often devastated. Co-workers feel as though their careers have been taken away from them and no-one in the company cares. They often suffer from anxiety, depression, a sense of betrayal, anger management problems as they become increasingly frustrated, broken relationships that do not stand up to the strain of work pressures, low self-esteem, and so on. What price does one place on human beings experiencing such things? Is it worth employing an organisational psychopath, even if they could make additional long-term financial profit for the company, when even one co-worker is going to experience these complaints as a result of the psychopath's behaviour? This is an ethical question that is left for the reader to decide based on their own value system. Shareholders and senior management may answer this question differently to those who would be working with the psychopath.

From a legislative perspective, each company has a duty of care to their employees to ensure that no personal harm is caused to them as a result of their work. In theory this precludes an organisational psychopath being employed in many cases. In practice, companies do not deliberately employ the organisational psychopath. Therefore the questions must be asked: should companies be doing more to detect organisational psychopaths entering their organisation, and should they implement policies that increase the probability of such psychopaths being detected and managed once they are working in an organisation? One final, but very important question concerns the rights of the organisational psychopath themselves. How does one achieve a balance between the rights of the psychopath and the rights of their victims not to be victimised? Is it discrimination to sack an employee solely on the grounds of having a personality disorder such as psychopathy? All of these questions must be answered before a solution to the issue of psychopaths in the workplace can be resolved.

10

Mistaken Identity?

FOR EVERY BAD manager, co-worker or client who is a workplace psychopath, there are many others who are not. In fact the majority of 'dysfunctional employees' are not psychopaths. There are a variety of alternative explanations for difficult or impossible workplace behaviours. Reasons can include lack of management/leadership training, low self-esteem, inability to cope with stress, inadequate communication skills, relationship/family problems, mental illnesses such as personality disorders, schizophrenia, and drug, alcohol or gambling addictions.

These alternate diagnoses still produce a manager, co-worker or client who makes life at work unbearable. The fact that the person is not a psychopath gives little comfort to the people experiencing the psychological and sometimes physical injury. Fortunately, many of the alternate diagnoses for dysfunctional workplace behaviour can be recognised and managed more easily than psychopathy.

Poor interpersonal skills – the over-controlling boss

One of the most common explanations for a manager or boss being mistakenly labelled a psychopath is poor interpersonal skills. Many managers who have poor interpersonal skills frequently 'over-control' their employees in an attempt to manage a situation they feel they have no control over. This over-control or 'intrusive supervision' alienates employees, which creates resentment, which causes the manager to become more and more frustrated about their lack of control over their staff. A vicious cycle is set up as the manager tries to re-assert their dominance, only to be faced with unhappy staff. Eventually either the manager cracks or the employees are transferred or resign after putting up with a great deal of physical and psychological stress.

David had worked for the government for 25 years, and he was finally promoted to a senior management position where he was responsible for 135 employees. He did not receive training in leadership or communication skills as it was assumed he had picked up these abilities throughout his 25 years of service.

In his first month as senior manager, he succeeded in alienating the majority of his employees as he attempted to assert his authority over the department. He changed their working hours without consultation, told employees he was not interested in their input. He said his department was not a democracy, giving orders to be followed not questioned. The employees complained to others which made David look like a bad manager who could not handle his staff. David reacted to this by clamping down even more, emphasising trivial rules and regulations that had not been followed for many years.

After David's boss reviewed his management style, it was suggested that David attend executive coaching and communication skills sessions. In these sessions David revealed that he was anxious about his new position, he had never been shown how to work with people because he had always experienced a hierarchical system in which employees 'followed orders'. Once he understood that over-controlling employees did not lead to productive workers, he was willing to change his approach.

> David now understands that leadership is not equal to control over people, but is about earning people's respect rather than demanding it.

Generally the over-controlling manager thinks about their employees and their job in a relatively predictable and limited way. Often they have a big workload (either in reality or in their own minds) and this causes them to feel tense, anxious and sometimes angry as they are not sure if they can cope. They sometimes resent the people who have given them the work. This resentment is often taken out on their subordinates.

Importantly, many over-controlling managers believe that all of the work has to be done perfectly by their employees because the quality of the work done is a direct reflection of their ability as a manager. If the work done by their employees is good, they look good as a manager and will get their next promotion. Therefore they reason that they have to monitor everything their employees do to guarantee that the work is perfect. Some of the thoughts that over-controlling managers have about their employees include:

- If I don't fight for people to do their work then nothing will get done.

- People can't be relied on to do the job right.
- If I don't stay right on top of them, it is going to be a complete and utter disaster.
- If this job is not done exactly how I want it done, it means that I am not a good manager.
- I don't have time to delegate jobs; it is faster to tell people how I want it done. That is what a manager does, isn't it?

Clearly these thoughts about employees and the work environment influence the over-controlling manager's behaviour. These thoughts also influence how the over-controlling manager interprets things that happen at work. When the over-controlling manager tells an employee how to do a job, and the job is then completed correctly, the over-controlling manager attributes this success to his or her management style. This means that in future they will continue to be over-controlling because it has worked in the past. Any resentment from their employees is interpreted as inability on the part of employees to cope with the stresses and pressures of their job. The over-controlling manager does not see that employee stress or reactionary behaviour might be caused by their own management style.

The over-controlling manager justifies his or her behaviour through the following beliefs about employees and appropriate workplace behaviours:

- You must know your place in the hierarchy; some day you too will be able to 'manage' other people.
- You must never challenge decisions I make about issues as this is costly and shows a lack of respect.
- You must not make decisions for yourself; employees cannot be trusted to do this until they have proven themselves, at which point they will be given a more senior role.
- Even though I delegate responsibility for certain things to you, everything you do showcases my ability as a manager, therefore I must personally approve everything that you do.

The beliefs held by the over-controlling manager need to be challenged, as does the validity of his or her conviction that they are the only person with the ability to complete a particular job. One of the most important aspects in this boss/employee relationship is the ability to communicate effectively. Communication skills such as the ability and willingness to listen, empathising with employees, and exchanging ideas clearly establishes a climate of trust.

Many managers and employees consider themselves to be good listeners, when the reality is usually the reverse. Some organisational psychologists claim that poor listening skills are the greatest source of conflict between managers and employees. Good listening involves thinking about what the other person is saying, asking relevant questions and reaching conclusions. The primary purpose of listening is to understand another person's point of view. If managers and employees worked toward this goal, and 'really' listened to each other, many conflicts could be avoided in the first place. A good psychologist should be able to coach a person in the art of effective communication.

The famous Type-A, B, C and D personalities

Different personality types often clash in the workplace, leading to conflict that has nothing to do with psychopathy. A major factor that differentiates between a personality clash from psychopathy is the psychopath's lack of remorse as well as experiencing pleasure from any psychological and/or physical injury caused to the victim.

There are many theories of personality, ranging from Freud's psychodynamic approach to Maslow's theory of self-actualisation and Skinner's behaviourism. One of the more popular theories used in the business world involves four personality types: A, B, C, and D. Not all personality types get along, and there are specific ways to deal with each personality type to help minimise workplace conflict.

The Type-A personality is a spontaneous, achievement driven person who is up-front, persuasive and a risk taker. This personality type is generally highly competitive and self-assured. People who work with these people may see them as aggressive and too competitive in going after what they want. The other traits of this type can often be interpreted as domineering, manipulative, pushy, impatient, arrogant and controlling. The Type-A personality dislikes people who are not fast and decisive, particularly those people who follow the rules to the letter. If you are working with or for a Type-A personality make sure positive feedback is given regularly and you are up-front and honest about what you want, you are always enthusiastic, recognise the importance of their work and encourage them to use their creative abilities.

The Type-B personality is a task-oriented person who must always win. This personality type takes charge and would describe themselves as practical, ambitious, methodical, efficient, direct, results-oriented, determined and conventional. The Type-B personality dislikes people who are ambiguous about what they want, who become emotional about practical matters, and people they believe are lazy. The Type-B personality can be seen by others as frugal, uncaring, distant, stubborn, aloof, uncompromising, and inflexible.

If you are working with or for a Type-B personality, make sure they are given as much control over their work as possible, are allowed to use their organisational abilities, are given challenging work, and their efficient and practical way of doing things is taken on board by co-workers. If they are your manager or boss, it is helpful to be clear and to the point, respect their authority, focus on results (these types want results rather than a long-winded explanation about why you could not finish something), follow their rules and regulations, and logically explain alternative ways of doing things.

The Type-C personality has a strong desire to help other people. This personality type keeps stress bottled up, and are often victims of the workplace psychopath rather than difficult employees to work with. They are generally trustworthy, enthusiastic, sensitive, approachable, good listeners, warm and outgoing, are often protective of people who are being victimised and want people to like them.

The Type-D personality is detail-oriented as opposed to having good interpersonal skills. They enjoy working alone, and can often be found in accounting, engineering, technical and other similar professions. They could be described as rigid, meticulous, accurate, strict rule followers and risk avoiders. Their approach could be characterised by people in conflict with them as boring, uninspiring, monotonous, anti-change, unsociable and a perfectionist. If you are working with or for the Type-D personality keep in mind that they respond to hard facts and data, consistency, detailed documentation of ideas and the work completed. They work within deadlines, and expect employees to do the same. They are also the type of person who will demand respect simply because they are the manager of a particular section.

No-one could figure out how Ian had got a managerial position in the public service. He seemed to have no personality and was rigid and difficult to get along with. He dismissed his employees' concerns without really listening to them. He applied the rules and regulations and did not tolerate his decisions being questioned. Ian rarely communicated verbally, he preferred to send his answers in the form of an official letter. This practice further alienated employees who 'answered to him'.

Ian was clearly of only average intelligence and had worked his way up to his present position through years of service rather than ability. He thought that his employees viewed him as an efficient and valuable member of the public service. He had no insight into the fact that his lack of social skills alienated the vast majority of employees. He was simply a Type-D personality who was so focused on getting the job done within the confines of a detailed set of rules that he did not think about how his social skills affected the people around him.

Passive-aggressive personality

Passive-aggressive people show a pattern of negative attitudes and passive resistance to demands for adequate performance in social and occupational settings. Passive resistance to working effectively can include such behaviours as forgetfulness, stubbornness, procrastination and intentional inefficiency or working deliberately slowly. These individuals channel their aggression into passive forms of resistance by slowing down the efforts of others, which is frustrating in many ways. The passive-aggressive personality can be quite difficult to detect, and many people do not know why they feel frustrated when dealing with these types because they do not do anything overt to cause this frustration. The passive-aggressive employee can be summed up as a person who obstructs the efforts of others by deliberately failing to do their share of work.

For example, a passive-aggressive employee may be given a presentation to prepare for their boss by a set date. The individual will not prepare the presentation, but will tell their boss it is ready right up until the day of the presentation. At this point, the boss is unable to give the presentation and looks like a failure.

The passive-aggressive person often feels cheated, unappreciated, misunderstood, always complaining to others about how overworked and underpaid they are. They frequently blame their failure on other people or the organisational systems, and may be sullen, irritable, impatient, argumentative, cynical and sceptical about everything. Authority figures often become the focus of discontent as the passive-aggressive person sees the authority figure as a significant cause of their problems. They may also resent people around them who do succeed. The passive-aggressive person may waver between open defiance and hostility toward an authority figure versus passive attempts to placate their supervisor by apologising and promising to improve their work performance. The passive-aggressive personality also likes to play win-lose games with others, and is always aiming to win as this makes them feel good about themselves and their ability.

Jane was an editor for a publishing house. She was always complaining about how overworked she was, constantly reminded her colleagues that she had too much work to review and too little time. When she was given a manuscript to work on, she would promise to deliver it by a certain time, and then fail to return the work by the promised date. She would tell management that the work required only small modifications and then at the last minute the manuscript would be returned with major changes that would take the author a considerable period of time to rework. In an industry working to very strict deadlines this was not appreciated, and people became frustrated with her. Her colleagues resented her behaviour as they ended up having to do a lot of the work she was responsible for. Jane vacillated between being extremely apologetic and pleading for people to be understanding versus open hostility towards colleagues for giving her so much work to do in the first place.

Narcissistic personality disorder

Sigmund Freud used the term narcissistic to describe people who showed an exaggerated sense of self-importance and a pre-occupation with receiving attention. The essential feature of narcissistic personality disorder is a pervasive pattern of grandiosity, the constant need for admiration and a lack of empathy for others.

Narcissistic people commonly overestimate their abilities and embellish their achievements, often coming across as boastful and conceited. They can become agitated or angry when people do not show them the respect and 'reverence' they believe they deserve. The narcissistic person fantasises about unlimited success, power, brilliance, beauty or idealised love. They also see themselves on par with famous people in terms of their achievements, and therefore expect to be treated the same as other 'stars'.

The narcissist believes that they are superior to other people and they boost their self-esteem by associating with people who are successful. For example, the narcissistic person will insist on having only the best doctor, lawyer, personal fitness instructor, hairdresser, membership of the best clubs, gyms, and so on.

The person with narcissistic personality disorder has a very fragile self-esteem because it revolves around constantly receiving admiration from other people. They like to show off their possessions to make others envious, and often openly seek compliments from people they are with. It is not unusual for them to unreasonably expect favourable treatment, such as being given the best table in a restaurant, parking wherever they want, or not having to line up to enter a nightclub. This sense of entitlement, combined with a lack of sensitivity to the wants and needs of others may lead to behaviour that exploits other people. However, this exploitation is not deliberately callous, it is simply a by-product of their need for admiration and special treatment. This fragile self-esteem makes the narcissistic person vulnerable to criticism from other people. Though they do not always show their feelings, criticism may leave them feeling empty, humiliated and degraded. They may react to criticism or perceived criticism with rage, counter-attack or disdain.

The narcissistic person does not have a great deal of success when it comes to recognising the desires and feelings of other people as they are too preoccupied with themselves and their own feelings. They often do not consider other people's needs, and frequently make insensitive remarks about a variety of things. For example, they may talk about how great their own health is to a person who is chronically ill in hospital.

The narcissist is often jealous of other people. They do not like it when people appear to be more successful than they are, believing that they should be the recipient of such success. They frequently minimise the contributions of other people who receive awards, and are described by others as arrogant and condescending.

Narcissistic personality disorder is estimated to occur in less than 1 per cent of the population. Of people with the disorder, about 50 to 75 per cent are males. They differ from the psychopath because their behaviour is driven by a need for admiration from other people as opposed to enjoyment of other people's suffering. Regardless of the different motivation, both the narcissist and the psychopath have the capacity to cause significant psychological damage to co-workers.

Jeremy was a lawyer in his early forties. He worked for a large law firm, and had all the trappings of success that went with his job – an expensive car, a house in an affluent part of the city and a series of attractive girlfriends (who did not go out with him for long at all). Jeremy described himself as a key player in the law firm (despite the fact he had been overlooked for partnership). He also exaggerated his achievements as a sportsman, indicating that when he finished school it was a difficult choice about whether to become a professional sportsman or a highly successful commercial lawyer. There was no evidence to support these claims.

Jeremy talked endlessly to colleagues about his visions of himself as a partner, making millions of dollars for the company and saving his clients from multimillion dollar law suits through his consummate skill as a lawyer. The reality was that Jeremy was not trusted by the law firm partners to handle anything more than routine, uncomplicated cases involving relatively small sums of money. Jeremy could not understand why he had been passed over for partnership, as he believed he was special. He told other people that the law firm was waiting for a big enough case to come along that would really use his skills.

Jeremy was also the cause of legal secretaries resigning or demanding transfers. He constantly looked for praise, and when it didn't happen he would became angry, taking it out on the legal secretaries, deliberately giving them too much work. He also blamed the legal secretaries for his own failure to produce work. His co-workers saw him as arrogant and condescending. When he was told that he was to work with an organisational consultant to develop a management plan, he agreed as he thought he was being groomed for a senior position. He insisted that the consultant be a well-recognised expert – that he 'only went to the best because winners attract winners'.

Histrionic personality disorder

Histrionic personality disorder refers to a condition where an individual is over-dramatic about everything and almost appears to be acting rather than genuinely experiencing things. People with histrionic personality disorder tend to be vain, extravagant and seductive. They often express emotion in an exaggerated way, such as sobbing uncontrollably at a sad movie or hugging someone they have just met as though they are long-lost friends. They are uncomfortable when they are not the centre of attention. They can be over-concerned about their looks and spend large amounts of money on clothing and jewellery.

The person with histrionic personality disorder is also fairly impulsive and has difficulty delaying self-gratification. They may have shallow and rapidly shifting emotions, while interaction with other people is often characterised by inappropriate sexually seductive or provocative behaviour. This provocative behaviour is not limited to relationships or close partners, it can be seen at work and on social occasions. They frequently consider relationships more intimate than they actually are.

Sufferers may seek to control people through emotional manipulation on one level, yet simultaneously they depend on them for attention on another level. They also have trouble with friends of the same sex as they are often seen as trying to 'steal' friends' partners through their provocative behaviour.

It is estimated that 2 to 3 per cent of the population may have the disorder. Males and females are equally likely to have histrionic personality disorder according to some studies. However these proportions are based on limited data.

The difference between histrionic personality disorder and psychopathy is that psychopaths manipulate for profit, power or other material gratification whereas histrionics manipulate to gain nurturance from those around them.

Don't jump to conclusions – over diagnosis and confirmatory bias

It is important to be aware of psychopathic behaviours and characteristics along with other extreme personality types to protect ourselves and to avoid conflict. However, it is equally important not to jump to conclusions or try to diagnose someone's behaviour without professional advice.

Misdiagnosis or improper use of a label is just as destructive for a person as a psychopath can be. There is a phenomenon known as confirmatory bias that is very important when it comes to people making judgements about whether a colleague is a workplace psychopath versus 'something else'.

Confirmatory bias is a term used in social psychology that refers to an error in how people make judgements about various situations. Generally speaking, confirmatory bias occurs where a person 'confirms' what they want to believe by selectively looking at certain bits of information available to them.

For example, a person may believe that they are working with a psychopath, therefore they read a book such as this one to find out more about the workplace psychopath. The person reads through all of the characteristics carefully, and then looks for those characteristics in their colleague. They try and remember behaviours that their colleague has done which fit the characteristics they have read about. They may remember that 'Bob had an affair 20 years ago with a secretary, therefore he is sexually promiscuous and fits that criteria', an incorrect conclusion. In effect they find what they want to find, and ignore any contradictory evidence. Confirmatory bias is very dangerous as it can lead to 'false positives'; concluding that a person is a workplace psychopath when in fact they are not.

It is important to remember in psychology (and science in general) that one must always try and disprove rather than prove a theory. There is a famous example used in science that illustrates why. If a scientist has a theory that 'all birds in the world are black', how does he or she go about validly testing that theory. There are two possibilities.

First, they can try and prove the theory by travelling the world and looking only for black birds, incorrectly concluding that their theory is true when they do not notice birds of any other colour because they are not looking for them.

Second, and more valid, is to travel the world and try to find a bird that is not black. In other words, the theory is tested by trying to disprove it rather than confirm it.

If a reader believes that they are working with a psychopath of any sub-type, they should go about trying to disprove rather than prove their 'theory'. If they cannot disprove their 'theory' that the person is a workplace psychopath because the person fits many of the characteristics after careful consideration of the evidence, then it is possible that the person they know may be a workplace psychopath. If the person does not fit sufficient characteristics, yet they are still 'dysfunctional' to work with, an alternate diagnosis may be more appropriate.

Regardless of the diagnosis, if the person is causing you to suffer in any way, it is important that you talk with people about the situation. This can be family, friends, or a professional. If you try and face the problem alone, and they are a workplace psychopath, you present a much easier target and will most likely suffer in the end.

Conclusion

IN MY WORK as a consultant, I have seen and continue to see the immense psychological devastation that workplace psychopaths inflict upon the people around them. The victim of a workplace psychopath is never the same again. Victims have a different perception of themselves, their lives, and certainly the workplace. Often they are isolated, withdrawn and hesitant to discuss their situation or allow other people into their life because the workplace psychopath has taught them to be afraid of such experiences. This is not to say they will be wounded forever, but they require a great deal of support and understanding from the people close to them before they can accept and move on from their negative experience.

While it does not surprise or shock me to encounter these victims and hear about the extent of the damage caused by workplace psychopaths, it does surprise me that very little or nothing has been done to address the problem, especially since awareness was raised with the publication of *Working with Monsters*. People talk about the topic and are fascinated by the notion that psychopaths can exist in workplaces. However, these same people are often unaware that people in their own workplaces, people they know, may be being isolated and victimised by a workplace psychopath. This is not a phenomenon that happens to 'someone else' – it may in fact be occurring in your own workplace. I have helped to unravel damage done to people targeted by workplace psychopaths, and I can tell you that most major companies, most government departments and a wide range of other organisations all have workplace psychopaths who are victimising people and destroying their lives as you read this book.

While books such as *Working with Monsters* and *The Pocket Psycho* raise awareness of the issue and empower targets and others to limit the workplace psychopath's ability to destroy people, this is not enough. Everyone should be aware of the tactics of the workplace psychopath and be prepared to do something about it when a workplace psychopath is identified. When we achieve this, workplace psychopaths will be unable to operate, because they rely on isolating their victims to destroy them. One of the greatest weapons the workplace psychopath uses is the indifference of others to the suffering of a colleague. It is often easier to ignore a problem at work than to become involved. What difference exists between the person who condones the workplace psychopath's behaviour by doing nothing about it and the workplace psychopath themselves? To what extent are we, as a society, responsible for the decision by Kate, the victim of a workplace psychopath we met at the opening of this book, to take her own life because she felt so helpless?

If you are – or think you are – being targeted by a workplace psychopath, talk to someone about it. Find out as much information as you can, and make sure you do not isolate yourself from the people who care about you. Ultimately, these are the people who will see you through the situation. In some cases it is also wise to seek professional help. Do not risk becoming another victim like Kate.

Acknowledgements

WRITING THIS BOOK could only be accomplished with the help of many people, to whom I am deeply grateful. First and foremost, I am indebted to the victims of workplace psychopaths who trusted me enough to share their experiences. They provided me with inspiration and an immense belief in the resilience of the human spirit to overcome all obstacles in the face of adversity. Similarly, the organisations that invited me to assess 'problem employees' must be thanked for their faith in me to preserve the confidentiality of our meetings and for allowing me to share their successful strategies for the benefit of employees and organisations experiencing similar problems.

Thanks also to the team at Random House. In particular, thanks to Jeanne Ryckmans for being so patient and believing in the idea of a second book about psychopaths in the workplace. Thanks to Julian Welch for his wonderful editing. It simply would not have been possible without your continued support.

Last, but certainly not least, I would like to thank my family and friends for being there for me over the years. Again, this book would not have been possible without your support, encouragement and love. I could not ask for more loving family and friends, and I am privileged to have all of you in my life.

References

Babiak, Paul (1995). 'When psychopaths go to work: A case study of an industrial psychopath', *Applied Psychology: An International Review*, Vol. 44, 171–188.

Babiak, P. and Hare, R. (2006). *Snakes in Suits*. New York: Regan Books.

Blackburn, R. (2000). *The Psychology of Criminal Conduct: Theory, Research and Practice*. Chichester: John Wiley & Sons.

Clarke, John and Shea, Andy (2001). *Touched by the Devil*. Sydney: Simon & Schuster.

Clarke, John (2005). *Working with Monsters: How to Identify and Protect Yourself from the Workplace Psychopath*. Sydney: Random House Australia.

Cleckley, Dr Hervey M. (1976). *The Mask of Sanity*. St Louis: Mosby, 5th ed. (original work published in 1941).

Hamer, M. (2001). 'Personality characteristics and superior sales performance', *Dissertation Abstracts International: Sciences and Engineering*, Vol. 62(5B).

Hare, Dr Robert D. (1991). *The Hare Psychopathy Checklist – Revised*. Toronto: Multi-Health Systems.

Hare, Dr Robert D. (1993). *Without Conscience: The Disturbing World of the Psychopaths Among Us*. New York: Pocket Books.

Ressler, R. and Schachtman, T. (1992). *Whoever Fights Monsters*. New York: St. Martin's Press.

Richards, Helene and Freeman, Sheila (2002). *Bullying in the Workplace: An Occupational Hazard*. Pymble, NSW: HarperCollins.

Also available from

RANDOM HOUSE AUSTRALIA

Working with Monsters
John Clarke

In this groundbreaking and comprehensive study, John Clarke explores the history and science of psychopathy, and pays particular attention to how and why psychopaths behave in organisations. *Working with Monsters* provides a fascinating insight into the mind of the workplace psychopath. Drawing on his studies and research into forensic psychology, and his experience in criminal profiling for law enforcement agencies as well as corporations experiencing difficulties with an employee, Clarke shows you how to recognise and manage a workplace psychopath in your midst.

The Gentle Art of Persuasion
Chester Porter QC

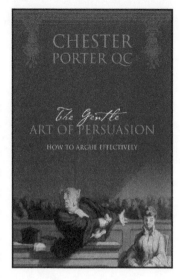

Much of life is spent arguing – at home, at work or for a living. Many arguments are futile wastes of time in which neither the participants nor the audience learn anything. Yet intelligent argument is often the only sensible way to advance our many causes, to spread knowledge and to achieve progress. It is one thing to sound impressive, to devastate the opposition or to make a great impression, but it is a greater challenge to change people's minds and convince them by your arguments. More often than not, real persuasion is achieved by quiet, rather than devastating, argument. In *The Gentle Art of Persuasion*, Chester Porter, the barrister and QC formally known as 'the Smiling Funnelweb', shares his brilliant advocacy skills, insight and years of experience to show you how to persuade an audience. With sound advice and wisdom from a man who has argued convincingly and effectively for the best part of his life – a man who can articulate ideas simply and without pomposity – this book is an indispensable tool for anyone who wishes to learn how to argue effectively.

Your Retirement
Anita Bell

How to plan, save and superannuate for financial independence

It seems that these days if the media isn't talking to us about our superannuation, they are telling us we will all be under-funded for our retirement. Not only do we now need to plan for self-funded retirement, with medical advances retirement is getting longer! Unless you want to spend thirty years eating baked beans on toast you need to get cracking now! In *Your Retirement* Anita Bell offers decade-by-decade strategies for investing money – in all the right places – as well as tips for goal setting and catch-up guides if you've been a bit busy focusing on the day-to-day to think of the future. Whether you are 16, 36 or 56, Anita shows you how to get cracking. Come on, no matter what your current circumstances, a little bit of time now will reap exponential rewards down the track. Covering superannuation, tax, allowances, investments in stocks, shares and property, plus loads of surprises, *Your Retirement* will give you the strategies and guides to look to the future with confidence. Whatever the lifestyle you aspire to in your future, Australia's debt-busting mum will set you on the path to financial independence.